AF256132

                              Airplane No. <u>0322</u>

PILOT'S HANDBOOK

for the

MODEL TBD-1 AIRPLANE

******
*****
***
*

*
***
*****
******

by Fred Plasma, Chief Technical Writer

DOUGLAS AIRCRAFT COMPANY, INC.

Santa Monica, California

-1937-

Copy No. 572

ISBN 978-1-935700-99-9

This text contains obselete information which
is presented solely for informational purposes.
It should not be used for any training program
involving aircraft.

Reprint ©2024 Periscope Film LLC
ISBN 978-1-935700-99-9

<u>FOREWORD</u>

This Handbook was prepared in strict accordance with Bureau of Aeronautics Specification SR-81. This book was not written in an attempt to provide a manual of flight instruction, but rather to offer the flying personnel a means of acquainting themselves with the many characteristic features of the TBD-1 airplane prior to their initial flight.

The ground covered here-in is limited to only that which is the concern of the pilot flying the airplane from the forward cockpit. The discussion includes a brief description of each control, the use of the controls, the take-off, flying and landing characteristics of the airplane, operating limitations, special precautions and operation charts and curves. The latter being accompanied by examples illustrating their correct usage.

More detailed information on the airplane in general, covering all features and installations with complete maintenance instructions will be found in the "Handbook of Erection and Maintenance Instructions" also furnished with the airplane.

TABLE OF CONTENTS

TABLE OF CONTENTS (CONT'D.)

TABLE OF CONTENTS (CONT'D.)

LIST OF ILLUSTRATIONS

TABLE OF CHARACTERISTICS

MODEL TBD-1

Normal Gross Weight - MK XIII
   Torpedo .... 9272#
Wing Area - Total .... 420 sq.ft.
Wing Span .... 50'-0"
Wing Loading - MK XIII
   Torpedo .... 22.0#/sq.ft.
Rated Power - 8000' Altitude .. 850 B.H.P.
Power Loading - MK XIII
   Torpedo .... 10.9#/H.P.
High Speed at Sea Level - MK
   XIII Torpedo .... 167 knots
High Speed at 8000' - 3-500#
   Bombs .... 179 knots
Stalling Speed - Sea Level -
   Flaps Up - MK XIII Torpedo .. 66 knots
Stalling Speed - Sea Level -
   Flaps Down - MK XIII Torpedo. 58 knots
Maximum Rate of Climb - Sea
   Level to 8000' - MK XIII
   Torpedo .... 870'/min.
Service Ceiling - 3-500#
   Bombs .... 20,000'
Take-Off Distance, MK XIII
   Torpedo - Sea Level - Calm .. 920'
Take-Off Distance, MK XIII
   Torpedo - Sea Level - 25
   knot Wind .... 355'
Cruising Speed at 60% Rated
   Power MK XIII Torpedo or
   3-500# Bombs .... 144 knots

Endurance at Cruising Speed at
  60% Rated Power at 8000'
    a. MK XIII Torpedo ....*1 hr. 43 min.
    b. 3-500# Bombs ....*2 hr. 39 min.
    c. 12-100# Bombs .... 3 hr. 49 min.
Renge at Cruising Speed at 60%
  Rated Power at 8000'
    a. MK XIII Torpedo ....*248 mi.
    b. 3-500# Bombs ....*381 mi.
    c. 12-100# Bombs .... 551 mi.
Endurance at High Speed at 8000'
    a. MK XIII Torpedo ....*1 hr. 0 min.
    b. 3-500# Bombs ....*1 hr. 32 min.
    c. 12-100# Bombs .... 2 hr. 13 min.
Range at High Speed at 8000'
    a. MK XIII Torpedo ....*179 mi.
    b. 3-500# Bombs ....*275 mi.
    c. 12-100# Bombs .... 392 mi.

*<u>Note</u>:

  1. These range and endurance figures are
in consideration of a <u>normal</u> fuel and oil
load as shown on pages 43 and 48 . Out of
this normal load, 27 gallons of fuel and
1 3/4 gallons of oil are allowed for warm-
up, take-off and landing.

  2. Provisional overloads (to extent of
tank capacity) in fuel and oil are allowed.
(See overload flight restrictions, page 75)

(Cont. Tabulation -
Flight, Power Plant)

SECTION I
COCKPIT ARRANGEMENT AND CONTROLS

A. General

1. The airplane is designed to be flown from the forward (pilot's) cockpit. However, the primary flight controls and several engine controls are duplicated in the second (assistant pilot's) cockpit so that the airplane may be flown from the latter position.

2. Several illustrations will be found on the following pages, identifying the controls in the pilot's cockpit.

B. Tabulation of Controls

1. Flight Controls

    a. Control Stick
    b. Rudder Pedals
    c. Aileron Tab
    d. Elevator Tab
    e. Rudder Tab
    f. Wing Flaps

2. Power Plant Controls

    a. Throttle
    b. Carburetor Mixture
    c. Carburetor Air Temperature
    d. Cowl Flaps
    e. Propeller Pitch
    f. Starter Engagement
    g. Ignition Switch

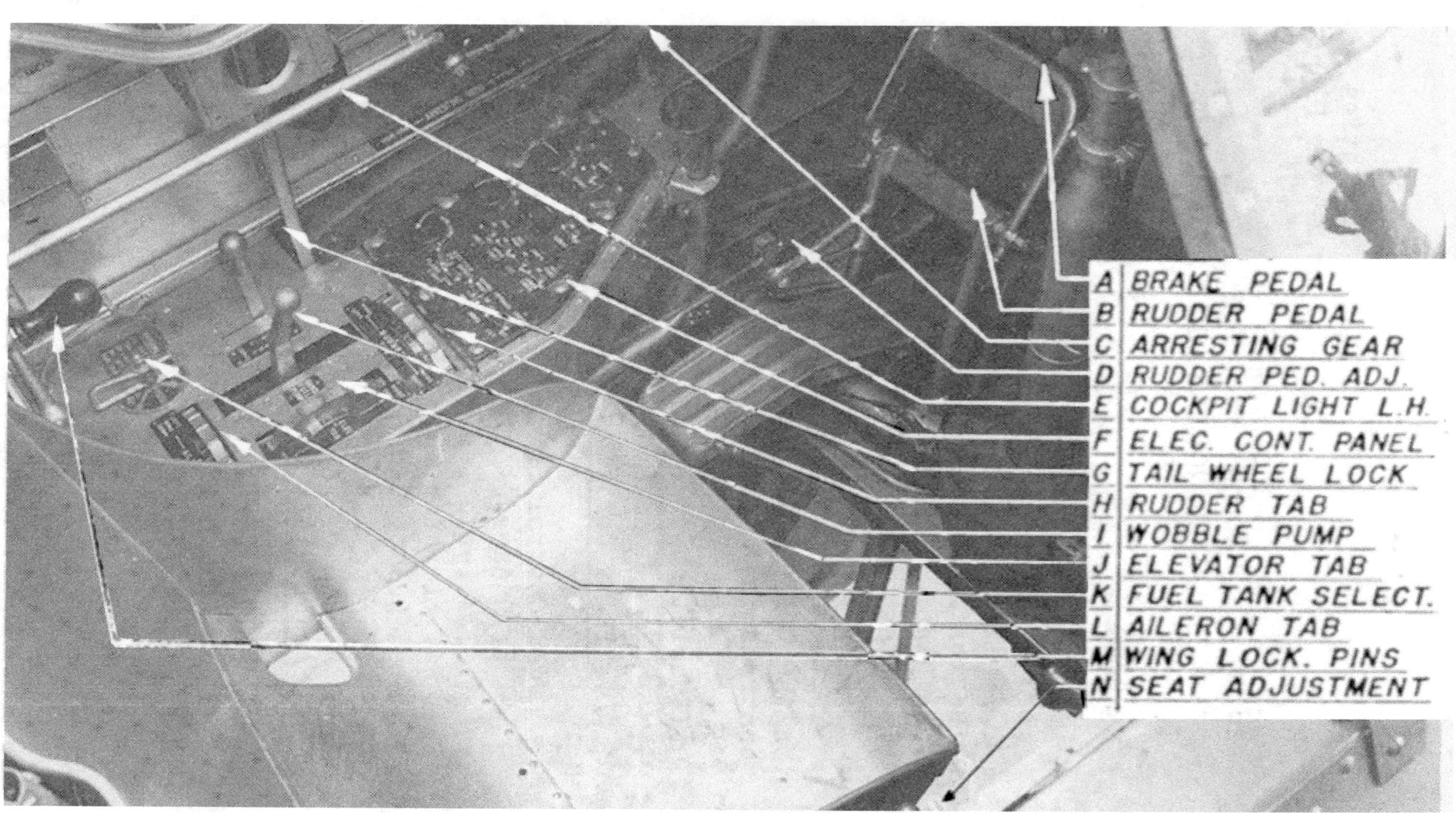

A BRAKE PEDAL
B RUDDER PEDAL
C ARRESTING GEAR
D RUDDER PED. ADJ.
E COCKPIT LIGHT L.H.
F ELEC. CONT. PANEL
G TAIL WHEEL LOCK
H RUDDER TAB
I WOBBLE PUMP
J ELEVATOR TAB
K FUEL TANK SELECT.
L AILERON TAB
M WING LOCK. PINS
N SEAT ADJUSTMENT

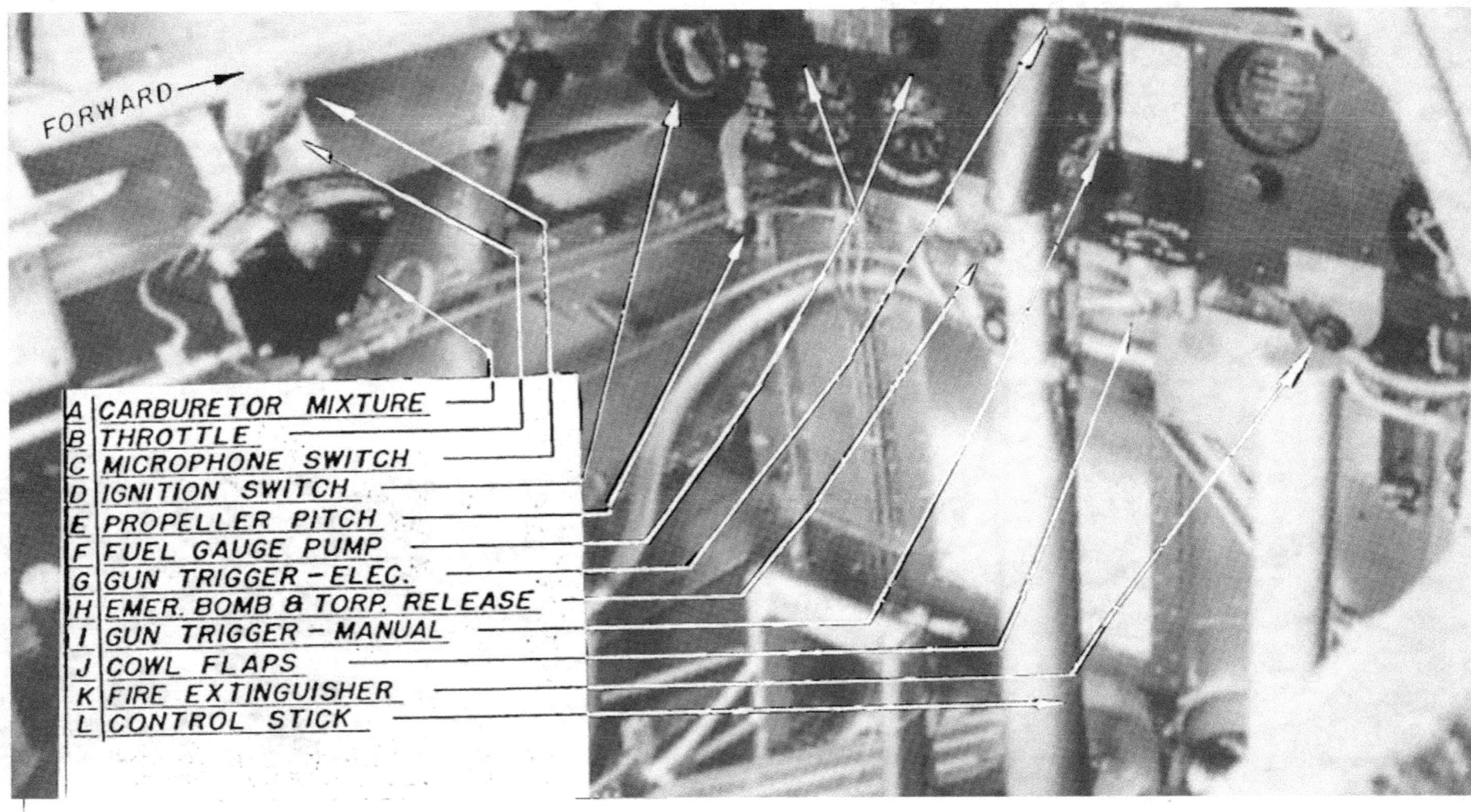

FORWARD
A CARBURETOR MIXTURE
B THROTTLE
C MICROPHONE SWITCH
D IGNITION SWITCH
E PROPELLER PITCH
F FUEL GAUGE PUMP
G GUN TRIGGER – ELEC.
H EMER. BOMB & TORP. RELEASE
I GUN TRIGGER – MANUAL
J COWL FLAPS
K FIRE EXTINGUISHER
L CONTROL STICK

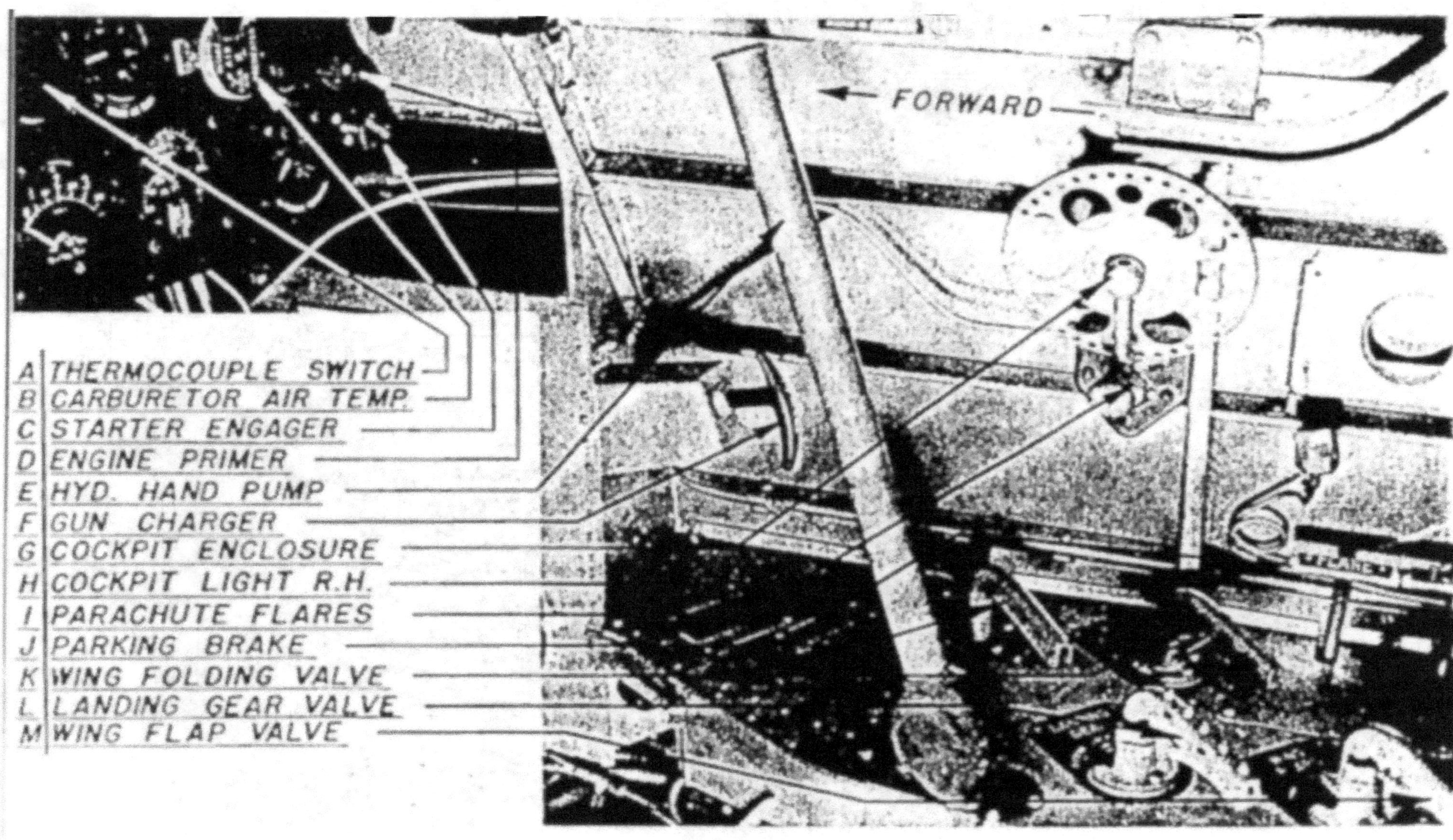

FORWARD
A THERMOCOUPLE SWITCH
B CARBURETOR AIR TEMP.
C STARTER ENGAGER
D ENGINE PRIMER
E HYD. HAND PUMP
F GUN CHARGER
G COCKPIT ENCLOSURE
H COCKPIT LIGHT R.H.
I PARACHUTE FLARES
J PARKING BRAKE
K WING FOLDING VALVE
L LANDING GEAR VALVE
M WING FLAP VALVE

(Cont. Tabulation -
Auxil., Useful Load)

    h. Primer
    i. Wobble Pump
    j. Thermocouple Switch

3. <u>Auxiliary Controls</u>

    a. Fuel Gauge Pump-L.H., R.H. Tanks
    b. Fire Extinguisher
    c. Flotation Gear
    d. Tail Wheel Lock
    e. Arresting Gear
    f. Rudder Pedal Adjustment
    g. Seat Adjustment
    h. Cockpit Enclosure
    i. Wing Locking Pins
    j. Wing Folding Valve
    k. Landing Gear Operating Valve
    l. Hand Hydraulic Pump
    m. Parking Brake
    n. Brake Pedals
    o. Electrical Control Panel
    p. Cock. Light Switch-L.H., R.H. Side
    q. Parachute Flares

4. <u>Useful Load Installation Controls</u>

    a. Torpedo Director
    b. Fixed Gun Charger
    c. Fixed Gun Trigger Release
    d. Microphone Switch
    e. Fixed Gun Switch-Safety Cover
    f. Torp. Release Switch-Safety Cover
    g. Gun Camera Switch
    h. Torp. and Emer. Bomb Release-Manual
    i. Oxygen Equipment

(Flight Controls -
Trim Tabs)

C. The Controls in Detail

1. Flight Controls

a. <u>Control Stick</u>
(1) Location: Conventional
(2) Reference: Item L, Page 5.
(3) Function: To operate Ailerons and Elevators providing lateral and longitudinal control.
(4) Operation: Conventional

b. <u>Rudder Pedals</u>
(1) Location: Conventional
(2) Reference: Item B, Page 4.
(3) Function: To operate Rudder providing directional control.
(4) Operation: Conventional

c. <u>Trim Tabs</u>
(1) Location: On mechanical control panel, L.H. side pilot's cockpit.
(2) Reference: Items H, J and L, Page 4.
(3) Function: To provide lateral, longitudinal and directional balance for the airplane with various loads and under various flight conditions. Tab position is given in degrees on the control wheel.
(4) Operation: Hand Mechanical
(a) Aileron
1a. <u>Left wing down</u> - turn control wheel <u>counter-clockwise</u> (outboard).
2a. <u>Left wing up</u> - turn control wheel <u>clockwise</u> (inboard).
(b) Elevator
1a. <u>Nose down</u> - turn con-

(Flight Controls -
Wing Flaps)

trol wheel <u>clockwise</u> (forward).

       2a. <u>Nose up</u> - Turn control
wheel <u>counter-clockwise</u> (aft).

      (c) <u>Rudder</u>

       1a. <u>Nose right</u> - Turn con-
trol wheel <u>clockwise</u> (inboard).

       2a. <u>Nose left</u> - Turn control
wheel <u>counter-clockwise</u> (outboard).

    d. <u>Wing Flap</u>

     (1) Location:

      (a) Control Valve - On hydraulic
control panel, R.H. side pilot's cockpit.

      (b) Position Indicator - Pilot's
upper instrument panel, R.H. side.

      (c) Hand Hydraulic Pump - On
hydraulic control panel, R.H. side pilot's
cockpit.

     (2) Reference: Item M, Page 6.

     (3) Function: To lower and raise
the wing trailing edge flaps providing, when
lowered, additional lift and drag at reduced
airspeed.

     (4) Operation: Hand Hydraulic

      (a) The control valve provides
for three positions: "DOWN", "LOCK" and "UP".
Following completion of the lowering or
raising operation, the control handle must be
returned to "LOCK". Should the pilot overlook
this step, and the engine is running, the
red warning light on the forward end of the
hydraulic panel will be illuminated, and, in
addition, the relief and by-pass valve beneath the hydraulic panel will operate causing considerable noise and vibration.

      (b) When the engine is running,
the flaps will be operated (raised or lowered)
immediately upon setting the control valve

(Flight Controls -
Wing Flaps)

to the position desired. When the engine is
stopped or pump has failed, however, the hand
hydraulic pump must be operated to build up
the necessary pressure.

NOTE: In operating the hand
pump, use slow, smooth, complete strokes.

(c) The indicator on the upper
instrument panel shows, in degrees ($0^{\circ}-45^{\circ}$),
the extent to which the flaps are lowered.
The indicator is controlled by cable from the
flap operating cylinder.

(d) TO LOWER FLAPS

1a. Move control lever to
"DOWN".

2a. Operate hand hydraulic
pump.

NOTE: When engine is run-
ning, this operation is eliminated.

3a. Watch position indica-
tor. When flaps reach desired position, move
control handle to "LOCK".

NOTE: CORRECT USE OF FLAPS IS IM-
PORTANT. INSTRUCTIONS COVERING USE AND LIMIT-
ATIONS ARE INCLUDED ON PAGES 57,58,67,70,81,84.

(e) TO RAISE FLAPS

1a. Move control to "UP".

2a. Operate hand hydraulic
pump until pumping becomes difficult.

NOTE: When engine is
running, this operation is eliminated.

3a. When indicator shows
flaps fully "UP" (0°), return control handle
to "LOCK".

NOTE: CORRECT USE OF
FLAPS IS IMPORTANT. INSTRUCTIONS COVERING USE
AND LIMITATIONS ARE INCLUDED ON PAGES 57,58,
67,70,81,84.

2. <u>Power Plant Controls</u>

   a. <u>Throttle</u>
      (1) Location: L.H. side pilot's cockpit.
      (2) Reference: Item B, Page 5.
      (3) Function: To control engine output.
      (4) Operation: Hand Mechanical
        (a) OPEN - FORWARD
        (b) CLOSE - AFT
        (c) A spring clip is incorporated in the throttle lever segment and serves as a "throttle stop". It is adjusted to a position indicative of the maximum allowable opening coincident with manifold pressure.
      NOTE: CORRECT USE OF THROTTLE IS OF PRIMARY IMPORTANCE. REFER TO INSTRUCTIONS AND LIMITATIONS ON PAGES 31-34,36,62,64.

   b. <u>Mixture Control</u>
      (1) Location: L.H. side pilot's cockpit (adjacent to throttle).
      (2) Reference: Item A, Page 5.
      (3) Function: To operate mixture regulating mechanism on carburetor compensating for varying flight conditions.
      (4) Operation: Hand Mechanical
        (a) RICH - FORWARD
        (b) LEAN - AFT
        (c) A segment at the extreme lean end of the sector is painted <u>red</u> to indicate the correct position of the control for stopping the engine. The control handle is equipped with a ratchet so that it may be locked in any position.
      NOTE: CORRECT USE OF MIXTURE CONTROL IS IMPORTANT. FOR DETAILED INSTRUCTIONS REFER TO PAGES 37,38,59,69,71.

(Power Plant Cont.-
Carb. Air Temp.)

c. <u>Carburetor Air Temperatures</u>
(1) Location: R.H. side pilot's lower instrument panel.
(2) Reference: Item B, Page 6.
(3) Function: To operate the valve in the carburetor air intake duct which varies the ratio of hot and cold air entering the carburetor. With the induction of warm air, ice formation is prevented or eliminated.
(4) Operation: Hand Mechanical
(a) <u>HOT Air</u> - Turn knob <u>counter-clockwise.</u>
(b) <u>COLD Air</u> - Turn knob <u>clockwise.</u>
(c) Rotary motion of the knob is transformed to linear motion through a reducer unit installed behind the instrument panel.
<u>NOTE</u>: CORRECT USE OF THIS CONTROL IS IMPORTANT. FOR DETAILED INSTRUCTIONS REFER TO PAGES 31,33,50-53,59,63,70,71.
d. <u>Engine Cowl Flaps</u>
(1) Location: Below pilot's instrument panel on centerline of airplane.
(2) Reference: Item J, Page 5.
(3) Function: To open and close cowl flaps, thereby regulating engine temperature.
(4) Operation: Hand Mechanical
(a) <u>Flaps OPEN</u> - Turn crank <u>counter-clockwise.</u>
(b) <u>Flaps CLOSED</u> - Turn crank <u>clockwise.</u>
(c) Rotary motion of the crank is transformed to linear motion through a reducer unit installed behind the instrument panel.

(Power Plant Cont.-
Prop Pitch, Starter)

NOTE: CORRECT USE OF THIS CONTROL
IS IMPORTANT. FOR DETAILED INSTRUCTIONS
REFER TO PAGES 38-41,59,63,71.

e. Propeller Pitch
(1) Location: L.H. side pilot's
lower instrument panel.
(2) Reference: Item E, Page 5.
(3) Function: To operate the controlling unit on the engine which, in turn,
shifts the blades to high or low pitch.
(4) Operation: Hand Mechanical
(a) HIGH PITCH - LEVER UP
(b) LOW PITCH - LEVER DOWN
(c) Instructions for use are
included on Pages 41,59,63,65,71.

f. Starter Engagement
(1) Location: R.H. side pilot's
lower instrument panel.
(2) Reference: Item C, Page 6.
(3) Function: To operate starter
clutch engaging inertia unit with engine,
and to engage booster magneto.
(4) Operation: Hand Mechanical
(a) After the inertia unit has
been energized sufficiently, it is connected to the engine crankshaft through a
clutch by use of the "STARTER" control.
(b) The booster magneto works
simultaneously with the starter engagement.
(c) TO ENGAGE STARTER
1a. Pull out and hold un-
til engine is running smoothly.
NOTE: PLUNGER MUST BE HELD
OUT UNTIL ENGINE IS RUNNING SMOOTHLY AS
BOOSTER MAGNETO IS IN OPERATION ONLY WHEN
STARTER IS ENGAGED.

g. Ignition Switch
(1) Location: L.H. side pilot's
lower instrument panel.

(Power Plant Cont.-
Ig. Switch, Primer)

(2) Reference: Item D, Page 5.
(3) Function: To make and break ground circuit to magnetos.
(4) Operation: By Hand
(a) Four positions are provided: "OFF", "LEFT", "RIGHT" and "BOTH". For normal operation, the switch is at "BOTH". "LEFT" and "RIGHT" are used for testing either phase of the dual ignition system.
(b) Switch "OFF" - Primary grounded.
(c) Switch "LEFT" - Left magneto and aft set of plugs in each row operating.
(d) Switch "RIGHT" - Right magneto and forward set of plugs in each row operating.
(e) Switch "BOTH" - Both magnetos and both sets of plugs in each row operating.
h. <u>Primer</u>
(1) Location: R.H. side pilot's lower instrument panel.
(2) Reference: Item D, Page 6.
(3) Function: To spray atomized fuel into cylinders #2, #3, #13 and #14 for cold weather starting (Refer to fuel system diagram, Page 44).
(4) Operation: By Hand, as a pump.
(a) The normal position of the primer when not in use is forward against the panel with the knob in the "OFF" position.
(b) TO PRIME ENGINE
1a. Turn knob to "ON" and pull out slowly.

(Power Plant Cont. -
Wobble Pump, Thermo. Sw.)

2a. Push plunger in <u>rapidly</u>, forcing fuel to cylinders.

3a. Repeat as required. Pulling out and returning is considered one stroke.

NOTE: INSTRUCTIONS COVERING NUMBER OF STROKES REQUIRED INCLUDED ON PAGE 32.

i. <u>Wobble Pump</u>

(1) Location: L.H. side pilot's cockpit.

(2) Reference: Item I, Page 4.

(3) Function: To provide fuel pressure prior to starting the engine and in the event of engine fuel pump failure.

(4) Operation: Hand Mechanical

(a) Moving the handle fore and aft operates the fuel pump building up pressure in the supply line to the carburetor (Refer to fuel system diagram, Page 44).

(b) A system of linkage connects the operating lever with the fuel pump. Instructions for using the wobble pump are to be found on Page 46.

j. <u>Thermocouple Switch</u>

(1) Location: R.H. side pilot's lower instrument panel.

(2) Reference: Item A, Page 6.

(3) Function: To connect, separately, cylinders #1, #3, #11 and #13 to the temperature indicator.

(4) Operation: By Hand

(a) Five switch positions are provided: "OFF" and a position for each of the four cylinder connections. When the switch is turned to any one of the cylinder connections, the indicator will immediately

(Auxiliary Controls -
Ga. Pumps, Fire Ext.)

register the temperature of that cylinder.

(b) When not in use, the switch should be "OFF". In flight it may be left on the hottest cylinder continually.

(c) CYLINDER TEMPERATURE LIMIT-ATIONS are discussed on the following pages: 35,39,40.

3. <u>Auxiliary Controls</u>

a. <u>Fuel Gauge Pumps</u>
(1) Location: L.H. side pilot's lower instrument panel.
(2) Reference: Item F, Page 5.
(3) Function: To clear the hydro-static cell and line of any fuel that may have accumulated there-in so that a true quantity reading may be taken.
(4) Operation: By Hand
(a) Pull knob out and release.
(b) Pulling the pump knob out fills the cylinder with air. When the knob is released, a spring returns the plunger to its "in" position, thereby forcing the air through the hydrostatic cell removing all fuel that had collected there.
NOTE: <u>DO NOT PUSH</u> PLUNGER IN. ALLOW IT TO RETURN OF ITS OWN ACCORD.
(c) For detailed instructions on use of pumps and gauges, refer to page 45.

b. <u>Fire Extinguisher</u>
(1) Location: Below pilot's lower instrument panel near centerline of air-plane.
(2) Reference: Item K, Page 5.
(3) Function: To operate the re-lease valve on top of the CO_2 cylinder.

(Auxiliary Controls -
Flotation Gear)

(4) Operation: Hand Mechanical
(a) TO RELEASE CO_2 - PULL
(b) The pull handle (painted
brown) is connected to the release mechanism by a flexible cable enclosed within a
fixed tube. Pulling the handle out (aft)
operates the mechanism releasing the CO_2
gas to the engine section.
c. <u>Flotation Gear</u>
(1) Location: R.H. side shelf between pilot's and assistant pilot's cock-
pits.

(2) Reference: Item k, Page 69.
(3) Function: To operate CO_2 releasing mechanism allowing gas to inflate
bags.

(4) Operation: Hand Mechanical
(a) TO INFLATE BAGS - PULL
handle.

(b) The pull handle (painted
blue-green) is connected to the release
mechanism by a flexible cable enclosed
within a fixed tube. Pulling the handle
operates the mechanism releasing the CO_2.
The gas under pressure operates the door
reléase cylinders, and then continues on to
inflate the bags.

(c) Automatic actuation of the
flotation gear, following a water landing,
is also provided with water pressure,
directed against a sensitized release
mechanism, being the operating agent. The
operation of the automatic release may be
delayed however, and, therefore, manual
release, if possible, is recommended.

(d) <u>IMPORTANT INSTRUCTIONS</u> for
the use of the flotation gear are included
on page 75.

(Auxiliary Controls -
Tail Wheel Lock, Arrest.Gr.

d. <u>Tail Wheel Lock</u>
(1) Location: On mechanical control panel, L.H. side pilot's cockpit.
(2) Reference: Item G, Page 4.
(3) Function: Engage and disengage tail wheel locking pin.
(4) Operation: Hand Mechanical
(a) TAIL WHEEL LOCKED - Control lever AFT.
(b) TAIL WHEEL FREE - Lever FORWARD and SECURED.
(c) In flight the wheel is always in a trailing position due to centering device.
(d) Instructions for using locking control for different take-off and landing conditions will be found on pages 59,71,72.
e. <u>Arresting Gear</u>
(1) Location: L.H. side pilot's cockpit.
(2) Reference: Item C, Page 4.
(3) Function: To lower and raise the arresting hook as necessary for carrier landings.
(4) Operation: Hand Mechanical
(a) HOOK DOWN - Handle AFT and SECURED.
(b) HOCK UP - Handle FORWARD and SECURED.
(c) A thumb operated lock secures the control in either of the two positions. A heavy coil spring installed in the "down" cable provides the necessary flexibility for the system.
(d) Instructions for use are included on page 71.

f. Rudder Pedal Adjustment

(1) Location: Adjacent to pilot's rudder pedals on forward ends of interconnecting rods.

(2) Reference: Item D, Page 4.

(3) Function: To accommodate pilot's of varying heights.

(4) Operation: By Hand. Adjustment works on a ratchet principle. Pulling up on the rod end allows the pedal to move free of the ratchet. After the pedal is relocated, the ratchet is released and secures the pedal in the new position.

g. Seat Adjustment

(1) Location: R.H. side pilot's seat.

(2) Reference: Item N, Page 4.

(3) Function: To disengage locking pins allowing seat to be raised or lowered.

(4) Operation: By Hand

(a) Moving the lever aft disengages the locking pins.

(b) A bungee is installed on the seat frame which tends to raise the seat. The pilot's weight is used to lower the seat.

h. Cockpit Enclosure

(1) Location: R.H. side pilot's cockpit.

(2) Reference: Item G, Page 6.

(3) Function: To open and close cockpit enclosure.

(4) Operation: Hand Mechanical

(a) Interior

1a. To Open - Pull cranking handle inboard and turn in clockwise direction. (Inboard pull must be maintained continually while cranking or locking

(Auxiliary Controls -
Cockpit, Wing Lock. Pins)

pin will engage disc.)

        2a. <u>To Close</u> - Pull cranking handle inboard and turn in counter-clockwise direction.

        (b) <u>Cockpit Ventilation</u> is provided by opening the enclosure to any one of the many locking pin positions.

        (c) Exterior

        1a. <u>To Open</u> - Depress button extending through skin on R.H. side of fuselage and move hood aft.

        2a. <u>To Close</u> - Depress button and move hood forward.

        (d) <u>NOTE</u>: <u>CAUTION</u>! HOOD OPENS RAPIDLY WHILE IN FLIGHT OR WHILE REVVING ENGINE ON GROUND. USE CAUTION!

    1. <u>Wing Locking Pins</u>

    (1) Location:

        (a) <u>Control Crank</u> - aft of pilot's seat on L.H. side of airplane.

        (b) <u>Indicators</u>

        1a. "Flag" or upper surface of L.H. and R.H. inner wing just inboard of hinge folding line near aft spar.

        2a. On control drum in pilot's cockpit.

    (2) Reference: Item M, Page 4.

    (3) Function: To retract (unlock) pins prior to folding and to extend (lock) pins following spreading of wings.

    (4) Operation:

        (a) UNLOCK - Pull crank knob forward and crank COUNTER-CLOCKWISE until "flags" are fully extended.

        (b) LOCK - Pull crank knob forward and crank CLOCKWISE until "flags" are fully retracted and winch shows "LOCKED".

(Auxiliary Controls -
Wing Lock. Pins, Wing Fold)

(c) Pilot's control unit incorporates a differentiating mechanism which permits one set of pins (L.H. or R.H.) to be withdrawn or engaged separately. <u>The winch may tend to stick after one set completes its travel</u>. Continue cranking until both indicator "flags" are fully extended or retracted and a definite stop is reached.

(d) The "flag" indicators are operated directly from the locking pins through a linkage system. The flags are painted red except for a narrow band of yellow at the top indicating that portion which normally (when locked) extends above the wing surface.

(e) The winch indicator consists of a cutout in the outer face through which the word "LOCKED" on a green background is visible when the pins are fully engaged.

(f) Following the spreading and locking operations check the following:

1a. Flags retracted with no red visible.

2a. Winch indicator showing "LOCKED".

3a. If above conditions are not satisfied, DO NOT ATTEMPT TO TAKE OFF.

j. <u>Wing Folding Controls</u>

(1) Location:

(a) Control Valve - Hydraulic panel, R.H. side pilot's cockpit.

(b) Hand Hydraulic Pump - Hydraulic panel, R.H. side pilot's cockpit.

(2) Reference: Items E and K, Page 6.

(3) Function: To fold and to spread outer wing panels.

(Auxiliary Controls -
Wing Folding)

(4) Operation: Hand Hydraulic

(a) The control valve provides for three positions "SPREAD", "OFF", and "FOLD". Following the completion of the spreading or folding operation, the control must be returned to "OFF". Should the pilot overlook this step, and the engine is running, the red warning light on the forward end of the hydraulic panel will be illuminated, and, in addition, the relief and by-pass valve beneath the hydraulic panel will operate causing considerable noise and vibration.

(b) When the engine is running, the wings will be operated (fold or spread) immediately upon setting the control valve to the desired position. When the engine is stopped, or pump has failed, however, the hand hydraulic pump must be operated to build up the necessary pressure.

NOTE: In operating hand pump, use slow, smooth, complete strokes.

(c) When the wings are in the folded position, there is considerable strain on the folding mechanism. To relieve this load, jury struts are provided to be installed in the special fittings on the wing tips and fuselage. The struts are stowed on the bulkhead behind the assistant pilot's seat.

(d) TO FOLD WING PANELS

1a. Release wing locking pins (Refer to Paragraph (4)   , Page 20).

2a. Move control valve to "FOLD".

3a. Operate hydraulic hand pump.

NOTE: When engine is running, this operation is eliminated.

(Auxiliary Controls
Ldg. Gr. Oper. Valve)

4a. When both wing panels are completely folded, return control valve to "OFF".

5a. Install jury struts.

(e) TO SPREAD WING PANELS

1a. Remove jury struts and stow behind assistant pilot's seat.

2a. Insure that locking pins are withdrawn.

3a. Move control valve to "SPREAD".

4a. Operate hydraulic hand pump.

NOTE: When engine is running, this operation is eliminated.

5a. When both wing panels are fully spread, return control valve to "OFF".

6a. Operate locking mechanism to extend pins to "LOCKED" position.

7a. Before taking off, check as follows:

al. Both locking pin indicator flags retracted and no red visible.

bl. Winch indicator showing "LOCKED" on green background.

k. Landing Gear Operating Valve

(1) Location:

(a) Control Valve - Hydraulic panel R.H. side pilot's cockpit.

NOTE: LANDING GEAR VALVE HANDLE IS PROVIDED WITH PROTRUDING STUDS FOR IDENTIFICATION BY TOUCH.

(b) Position Indicator - R.H. side pilot's upper instrument panel.

(c) Warning Signals - L.H. and R.H. side pilot's upper instrument panel.

(2) Reference: Item L, Page 6.

(Auxiliary Controls -
Ldg. Gr. Oper. Valve)

(3) Function: To extend and retract the main landing gear.

(4) Operation: Hand Hydraulic

(a) The control valve provides for three positions "EXTEND", "LOCK" and "RETRACT". Following completion of the extending or retracting operation, the control must be returned to the "LOCK" position. Should the pilot overlook this step, and the engine is running, the red warning light on the forward end of the hydraulic panel will be illuminated, and, in addition, the relief valve beneath the hydraulic panel will operate causing considerable noise and vibration.

(b) When the engine is running, the landing gear will be operated (extend or retract) immediately upon setting the control valve to the desired position. When the engine is stopped, or pump has failed, however, the hand hydraulic pump must be operated to build up the necessary pressure.

NOTE: In operating hand pump, use slow, smooth, complete strokes.

(c) The mechanical indicator system is connected through chain and cables to operating linkage on each landing gear assembly. The operation is positive.

(d) The electrical warning signals comprise an illuminated sign on the R.H. side of the upper panel, with the warning "CHECK WHEELS" and a red jeweled light on the L.H. side. A switch is installed adjacent to, and is operated from the landing gear brace strut. A second switch is operated from the throttle control. The warning signals and their identification are listed below:

(Auxiliary Controls
Hydraulic Pump)

1a. SIGNALS OFF - Landing
gear retracted and throttle in cruising position.

2a. SIGNALS OFF - Landing
gear extended and throttle in any position.

3a. SIGNALS ON - Landing
gear retracted and throttle closed to 1200
r.p.m. or less (adjustment available).

(e) TO RETRACT GEAR

1a. Move control handle to
"RETRACT" position.

NOTE: Wheels will be
blown back about midway by air pressure;
hesitate several seconds and then continue
upward as hydraulic pressure builds up.

2a. Operate hand hydraulic
pump.

NOTE: When engine driv-
en pump is operating, this step is eliminated.

3a. When indicator shows
both (L.H. and R.H.) gears fully "UP", return control handle to "LOCK".

(f) TO EXTEND GEAR

1a. Proceed as indicated
under Paragraph (e) preceding, except move
control handle to "EXTEND".

1. Hand Hydraulic Pump

(1) Location: Hydraulic panel, R.H.
side pilot's cockpit.

(2) Reference: Item E, Page 6.

(3) Function: To build up pressure
within the hydraulic system when the engine
driven pump is inoperative.

(4) Operation: By Hand

(a) Peak efficiency is obtained
from the pump when it is operated using a
full, smooth stroke.

(Auxiliary Controls -
Brake Control, Pedals)

m. <u>Parking Brake Control</u>
(1) Location: Hydraulic panel, R.H. side pilot's cockpit.
(2) Reference: Item J, Page 6.
(3) Function: To lock wheel brakes, thus preventing airplane from rolling.
(4) Operation: Hand Mechanical.
(a) The parking handle operates a ratchet installed on the brake cylinder. With the handle to the "LOCK" position, the ratchet is engaged and locks the brake operating cylinder in the "brakes on" position.
(b) The parking handle is automatically released when the brake pedals are pressed.
(c) TO LOCK BRAKES FOR PARKING
1a. Depress (toe) brake pedals.

2a. Move handle to "PARK".
3a. Release pedals while holding parking handle in "PARK" position.
<u>NOTE</u>: The parking brake is provided primarily for starting and warming the engine and for short parking periods. Wheel chocks are recommended for extended parking periods.
(d) TO RELEASE PARKING BRAKE:
1a. Depress brake (toe) pedals.

2a. Handle will return to "FREE" position.
n. <u>Brake Pedals</u>
(1) Location: Installed on upper end of each rudder pedal.
(2) Reference: Item A, Page 4.
(3) Function: To operate wheel brakes.

(Auxiliary Controls -
Electrical Panel)

   (4) Operation: By left and right
foot.

    (a) Brakes are operated hy-
draulically from individual master cylinders independent of the major hydraulic
pressure system. Hydraulic fluid, however,
is supplied from the main reservoir.

    (b) TO APPLY BRAKES - depress
toe pedals.

    (c) Brakes operate independent
of rudder pedal action.

    (d) TO RELEASE BRAKES - remove
pressure from toe pedals.

    o. Electrical Controls Panel

    (1) Location: On horizontal panel,
L.H. side pilot's cockpit.

    (2) Reference: Item F, Page 4.

    (3) Function: To operate panel
lights, navigation lights, landing light,
fixed gun, torpedo release, etc.

    (4) Operation: By Hand

    (a) Panel comprises toggle
switches and rheostats. The torpedo release
and machine gun switches have safety covers
to protect against accidental discharge.

    NOTE: This (pilot's) panel
does not include any switches providing for
control of the main battery and generator
distribution lines. These switches are located on the electrical panel in the gunner's (rear) cockpit. (Refer to "Handbook
of Erection and Maintenance Instructions"
for information concerning main line
switches).

    (b) A supply socket with its
independent switch is provided for acces-
sory equipment.

(Auxiliary Controls -
Cock. Lts., Flares)

    p. <u>Cockpit Lights</u>

        (1) Location: L.H. and R.H. sides of pilot's cockpit.

        (2) Reference: Items E and H, Pages 4 and 6.

        (3) Function: To light mechanical and hydraulic control panels.

        (4) Operation: By Hand

    q. <u>Parachute Flares</u>

        (1) Location: Aft of hydraulic panel on R.H. side of pilot's cockpit.

        (2) Reference: Item I, Page 6.

        (3) Function: To operate flare release mechanism.

        (4) Operation: Hand Mechanical

            (a) Each of the two flare cannisters has its independent release mechanism, operated through a system of cables and linkage.

            (b) TO RELEASE FLARES

              1a. Pull handle and hold several seconds.

  4. <u>Useful Load Installation Controls</u>

    a. <u>Torpedo Director</u>

        (1) Location: Above pilot's upper instrument panel near centerline of airplane.

        (2) Function) Refer to Bureau of
        (3) Operation)
Aeronautics Specifications.

    b. <u>Fixed Gun Charger</u>

        (1) Location: Above forward end of hydraulic panel, R.H. side pilot's cockpit.

        (2) Reference: Item F, Page 6.

(3) Function)
(4) Operation): Refer to Bureau of
Aeronautics Specifications.

    c. <u>Fixed Gun & Gun Camera Elec. Release</u>

      (1) Location: Top of control stick.

      (2) Reference: Item G, Page 5.

      (3) Function)
      (4) Operation): Refer to Bureau of
Aeronautics Specifications.

    d. <u>Fixed Gun & Gun Camera Man. Release</u>

      (1) Location: Grip on top of con-
trol stick.

      (2) Reference: Item I, Page 5.

      (3) Function)
      (4) Operation): Refer to Bureau of
Aeronautics Specifications.

    e. <u>Microphone Switch</u>

      (1) Location: Top of throttle con-
trol, L.H. side pilot's cockpit.

      (2) Reference: Item C, Page 5.

      (3) Function)
      (4) Operation): Refer to Bureau of
Aeronautics Specifications.

    f. <u>Fixed Gun Master Switch</u>

      (1) Location: Electrical control
panel, L.H. side pilot's cockpit.

      <u>NOTE</u>: Safety cover over switch.

      (2) Reference: Item F, Page 4.

      (3) Function)
      (4) Operation): Refer to Bureau of
Aeronautics Specifications.

    g. <u>Torpedo Release Switch</u>

      (1) Location: Electrical control
panel, L.H. side pilot's cockpit.

      <u>NOTE</u>: Safety cover over switch.

      (2) Reference: Item F, Page 4.

      (3) Function)
      (4) Operation): Refer to Bureau of
Aeronautics Specifications.

(Use. Load Insta. Cont. -
Armament)

h. <u>Gun Camera Master Switch</u>
(1) Location: Electrical control
panel, L.H. side pilot's cockpit.
(2) Reference: Item F, Page 4.
(3) Function)
(4) Operation): Refer to Bureau of
Aeronautics Specifications.
i. <u>Torpedo and Emergency Bomb Release</u>
(1) Location: Pilot's lower instrument panel, near centerline of airplane.
(2) Reference: Item H, Page 5.
(3) Function:
(a) To drop torpedo manually.
(b) To clear all bomb racks in
an emergency.
(4) Operation:
(a) TO DROP TORPEDO - PULL
(b) TO CLEAR BOMB RACKS - PULL
<u>CAUTION</u>: Do not operate emergency
bomb release while ballast is being carried
on aft bomb rack.
j. <u>Oxygen Equipment</u>
(1) Location: R.H. side pilot's
cockpit.
(2) Function: To provide oxygen to
flight personnel for high altitude operation.
(3) Operation:
(a) Instructions covering NOR-
MAL and EMERGENCY use of the oxygen equipment are included on the face of the regulator unit.
(b) WARNING: Equipment will
function normally until supply cylinder is
nearly empty. Pressure range is 2000 lbs.
per square inch (full) to about 300 lbs.
per square inch (nearly empty).

SECTION II

POWER PLANT OPERATION

A. Engine

1. Model Specification

    a. Pratt & Whitney, Model R-1830-64
    b. Geared - 3:2
    c. Blower Ratio - 11.9:1
    d. Compression Ratio - 6.5:1
    e. Rating (Standard Atmosphere)
       (1) Normal - 850 B.H.P. at 2450
r.p.m. at 35.5" Hg. at Sea Level
       (2) Normal - 850 B.H.P. at 2450
r.p.m. at 8000' at 32.5" Hg.
       (3) Take-Off - 900 B.H.P. at
2500 r.p.m. at 37" Hg.
    f. Cylinder Numbers (in direction of
propeller rotation.
       (1) Front Row - 2,4,6,8,10,12,14
       (2) Rear Row - 1,3,5,7,9,11,13
    g. Fuel - 87 Octane as of Navy Speci-
fication M-222 or M-302.

2. Starting

    a. Set parking brake.
    b. Check fuel and oil supply.
    c. If engine has been standing idle
for four hours or more, pull it through
several revolutions by hand to clear cylinders of any accumulation of fuel and oil.
    d. Open cowl flaps.
    e. Turn carburetor heat control to
"COLD".
    f. Turn tank selector to "RIGHT".

g. Move propeller pitch control up to "HIGH PITCH".

h. Set mixture control to "RICH".

i. Work wobble pump as required to maintain a pressure of three pounds (3#) on gauge during starting operation.

j. Operate primer

(1) 6 to 8 strokes when engine is cold.

(2) 2 to 4 strokes when engine is warm.

k. Move throttle through complete range 3 to 5 times and set at 1/3 open.

l. Energize inertia starter by hand crank.

m. Turn ignition switch "ON".

n. Engage starter. <u>Hold plunger out until engine is running smoothly.</u>

o. Maintain engine revolutions as low as possible until oil pressure shows on gauge; this usually requires from 15 to 30 seconds. When pressure registers on gauge, immediately increase r.p.m. to 800-1000.

<u>WARNING:</u> DO NOT PUMP THROTTLE. Excessive pumping when engine is cold is the frequent cause of backfire with its accompanying fire hazard.

p. After the engine has started and is operating at 800-1000 r.p.m., proceed to warm it, observing the instructions on the following page.

3. <u>Starting Precautions</u>

a. Insure that propeller is in HIGH PITCH before starting engine.

b. In extremely cold weather if difficulty is experienced in starting, the idle adjustment may be moved to the rich side.

c. If the engine does not start immediately, do not continue priming. Excessive priming washes the oil film from the cylinder walls which is likely to cause scoring of the pistons and cylinders.

d. Hard starting is sometimes caused by leaky primer lines and primer pump packing. If there is doubt as to whether or not the primer is supplying fuel to the cylinders, remove a line from one cylinder and observe the result when the pump is operated. Considerable fuel should be sprayed from the open line.

e. If there is evidence that the engine is flooded, it will be necessary to clear the cylinders and induction system of the excess fuel.

(1) Open throttle WIDE.

(2) Pull engine through four or five revolutions turning in normal direction (Do not turn backward).

f. Oil pressure should build up and register on gauge immediately after engine starts. If there is no indication of oil pressure after thirty seconds (30 sec.), STOP the engine and check for trouble.

4. <u>Warming Up</u>

a. When atmospheric conditions are favorable for carburetor icing, (high humidity), use one to three turns of heat control to maintain carburetor air temperature at approximately 32°C.

b. Run engine between 800 and 1000 r.p.m. until oil inlet temperature has reached at least 30°C. with a pressure reading of 30 to 40 pounds.

c. Engine should not be revved up (above 1000 r.p.m.) until cylinder head temperatures are at least 120°C.

d. After the minimum temperature conditions given in Paragraphs b and c, preceding, are reached, open the throttle, not to exceed 30" Hg. manifold pressure, for flash run and test ignition in the usual manner. At no time may cylinder head temperatures exceed 260°C. During flash run, check the following:

(1) R.P.M. drop on one magneto not to exceed 100 R.P.M.

(2) Oil pressure - 70-90 pounds.

(3) Fuel pressure - 4-5 pounds

e. The minimum allowable oil pressure while idling is 15 pounds.

f. The engine is sufficiently warmed for safe take-off when the following conditions exist:

(1) Oil inlet temperature -40-70°C.

(2) Cylinder head temperature - 150-200°C.

g. <u>CAUTION</u>: Do not idle engine below 800 r.p.m. while on the ground. At slow speeds the spark plugs are easily fouled, and, inasmuch as the ignition may not be checked again before take-off, this condition would not become evident until then. A fouled plug during take-off may cause disaster as detonation and loss of power would occur.

(Engine -
Prop. Oper. Cond., Stop.)

5. Proper Operation Conditions

Condition	Min	Max	Desired
Oil Inlet Temp. - Take-Off	40°C.	85°C.	60-70°C.
Cylinder Temp. - Take-Off - 5 Min.	150°C.	290°C.	235-260°C.
Cylinder Temp. - Climb		260°C.	200-235°C.
Cylinder Temp. - Continuous Cruising		235°C.	200°C.
Oil Pressure - Idling	15#		
Oil Pressure - Cruis.	50#	100#	70-90#
Fuel Pressure - Idling	2#		
Fuel Pressure - Above 1200 r.p.m.	4#	6#	5#
Carburetor Air Intake Temperature		42°C.	32-35°C.

6. Stopping

a. Before engine is stopped, place propeller control in "HIGH PITCH" position.

b. Turn carburetor heat control to full "COLD".

c. Set mixture control to full "LEAN" (aft end of quadrant painted red indicating correct position for stopping engine).

NOTE: If engine continues to fire with mixture control in full lean position, check primer shut-off valve for leak.

(Manifold Pressure)

    d. Move ignition switch to "OFF" after engine has stopped.

B. <u>Manifold Pressure</u>

    1. In order to increase engine output for high altitude operation, a supercharger is incorporated in the engine. At low altitudes however, the engine cannot withstand the maximum pressure output from the supercharger. Therefore, the use of the throttle must be restricted to hold the manifold pressure within allowable limitations. A throttle stop is provided and adjusted to limit sea level takeoff to 37" Hg. Throttle may be held to stop only until the airplane is well off the ground (5 minutes maximum duration) at which time it is returned to a position limiting manifold pressure to 34.5" Hg. and r.p.m. to 2450. For take-off from altitude fields, stop may be ignored and throttle opened to give 37" Hg.

    2. A table showing various limitations for "Maximum Allowable Power Operation" will be found on Page 61. <u>NOTE</u>: Engine r.p.m. or manifold pressure must never exceed the maximum allowable for a given flight condition. Should the limitation be exceeded, reduce throttle setting.

    3. If the recommended normal climbing speed (85-90 knots from Sea Level to 8000' at 2450 r.p.m. in low pitch) is exceeded at limiting manifold pressure near rated altitude (8000'), it is probable that the maximum r.p.m. (2450) will be exceeded. This must not be done.

(Mixture Control

4. For cruising and similar conditions of operation, the throttle, manifold pressure and r.p.m. must be reduced. The table on Page 64 shows the <u>maximum allowable</u> conditions for continuous cruising operations based on 600 B.H.P. (70% rated power). It is recommended that the airplane be operated at 65% (or less) rated power (Refer to Cruising Charts, Pages 86-89) because under this condition the efficiency of the airplane is increased and, in addition, the mixture may be leaned to "lean best power" (20 R.P.M. drop) setting. The influence of these two factors brings the fuel consumption down to approximately 45 gallons per hour.

C. Mixture Control

1. Instructions for using the mixture control are given in terms of:

a."Rich Best Power" - As the mixture is leaned from a full rich position, the r.p.m. should increase 5, 10 or more. The point at which this maximum r.p.m. value is first noted is called "rich best power".

b. "Lean Best Power" - Further leaning from the "rich best power" setting will eventually cause a drop in r.p.m. The point at which the r.p.m. begins to fall is called "lean best power".

c. "Best Power" - The range of maximum r.p.m. between "rich best power" and "lean best power" is called "best power".

2. Because of the many variables that enter into each flight, the mixture control should be checked frequently. Indication of

(Mixture Control -
Adjustment)

the need for adjustment of the mixture control is shown by changes in r.p.m., provided the throttle setting and flight path are undisturbed. Use of mixture control at <u>any time</u> is contingent upon satisfactory engine cooling.

3. <u>Adjustment</u>

a. <u>Operation ABOVE 85% RATED POWER</u>
(1) At altitudes from Sea Level to 4000' - Mixture "Full Rich".
(2) At altitudes above 4000' - Lean only enough to maintain smooth engine operation.
b. <u>Operation BETWEEN 70% and 85% RATED POWER</u>
(1) At any altitude - Set mixture at "Rich Best Power".
(2) Watch cylinder temperature. Maximum allowable for continuous operation is 260°C.
c. <u>Operation BELOW 70% RATED POWER</u>
(1) At any altitude - Mixture may be leaned to give drop of 20 r.p.m. in engine speed. Watch cylinder temperature. Recommended maximum for cruising operation is 235°C.
(2) This is the condition of minimum fuel consumption.

D. <u>Engine Cowl Flaps</u>

1. The use of the cowl flaps is the principal means of controlling cylinder temperature. However, the use of the cowl flaps to reduce excessive cylinder tempera-

(Engine Cowl Flaps)

ture resulting from too lean mixture must be avoided. In general, the flaps should be set as follows:

     a. Starting, Warm-Up and Taxiing - FULLY OPEN.

     b. Take-Off - OPEN only to hold maximum to $290^{\circ}C$. (5 min. only).

     c. Climbing - OPEN only to maintain $235-260^{\circ}C$.

     d. Cruising and Similar Level Flight - CLOSED.

     e. Diving - CLOSED.

2. The cowl flap position should be adjusted to suit the flight and air temperature condition so that the normal maximum cylinder temperature for that particular operating condition is not exceeded (Refer to table of cylinder temperatures, Page 40).

3. Opening the flaps increases the drag of the airplane. Therefore, it is desirable to have them closed as much as possible. This is not serious in climb, however, as the airspeed is low and the rate of climb but little affected by the opened flaps. From a standpoint of obtaining the maximum of service from the engine, the flaps should be opened as necessary, regardless of a possible decrease in performance.

E. Cylinder Temperatures

1. The airplane is provided with a four point thermocouple system to cylinders #1, #3, #11 and #13. The following table gives

(Cylinder Temperature)

temperature limitations. Check the cylinder temperatures systemmatically, especially when operating the airplane under critical conditions. The switch may be left on the hottest cylinder during flight.

CYLINDER TEMPERATURES IN DEGREES CENTIGRADE ($^{\circ}$C) FOR VARIOUS CONDITIONS

Condition	Max	Min	Desired
Warm-up, before revving engine for flash run		120	150
Ground running	235		150-200
Before take-off	235	150	150-200
Take-Off	290*		235-260
Climbing	260		200-235
Cruising	235		200
Gliding		120	150-200

*This temperature allowable for 5 minutes duration, ONLY.

2. Cylinder temperatures in climb are practically unaffected by manifold pressures. Temperatures in climb at low pressures, part throttle, (20"-25" Hg.) will be substantially the same as those at limiting manifold pressure.

3. The speed of the airplane in climbing is an important factor in respect to

(Propeller -
Make, Blade Set.)

cylinder temperatures. Prolonged steep
climbing at low airspeed may result in high
temperatures. Under severe operating conditions it will be found desirable to climb
at airspeeds slightly higher (90 to 95 knots)
than that for best climb in order to obtain
adequate cooling. An increase in airspeed
while climbing of 5 knots will reduce cylinder temperatures considerably with very little sacrifice in rate of climb.

F. Propeller

   1. Make:

      a. Hamilton Standard, 3-blade
         Design - 6111A-6
         Hub - #N27310
         Blades - #N61563, N61564, N61565
      b. Diameter - 11'-0"
      c. Pitch Range - 10° @ 42" radius

   2. Blade Settings

      a. Propeller blade settings are nec-
essarily a compromise between best take-off
performance and best "all-around" performance. The lowest pitch setting (17° at 42"
radius) that will hold the engine to 2500
r.p.m. at 37" Hg. manifold pressure at sea
level is the setting of maximum performance
for take-off. In climbing, however, the
performance is greatly reduced since at
normal climbing airspeed (85 to 90 knots
indicated), it will be necessary to operate
at lower manifold pressure in order to hold
the engine to 2450 r.p.m. Under the same
conditions of low pitch setting, if the

blades are moved to "HIGH" pitch for climbing operation following take-off, the engine may be operated at the normal climbing manifold pressure, but the r.p.m. will be greatly reduced, and, therefore, the rate of climb, likewise, will fall off.

b. It is obvious that the use of the low pitch setting of 17° must be confined to special cases where maximum take-off performance is necessary.

c. The following settings are considered normal for the best all around airplane performance:

Low Pitch - 19°
High Pitch - 27°

G. Fuel System

1. Tanks

a. The two fuel tanks are located in the L.H. and R.H. inner wing panels. The tanks are filled through the opening in the upper surface. Each tank has a capacity of 90 gallons. The L.H. tank has a reserve of 27 gallons. The various fuel loads carried are given in the table following.

2. Selector Valve

a. The tank selector valve is to be operated as indicated on the chart, following.

b. When operating on "LEFT" tank, fuel may be obtained down to 27 gallon reserve supply.

c. CAUTION: When the reserve fuel is used for take-off, be sure to switch to right or left tank immediately following initial

TABLE OF FUEL LOADING

ARMAMENT LOADING CONDITION	SMOKE SCREEN LAYER	TORPEDO	BOMBER	
			3-500#	2-500# 1-1000# 12-100#
Gallons of Fuel Carried	180	96*	133*	180

*Normal fuel load. Capacity load allowed
with flight restrictions. See page 76.

USE OF SELECTOR VALVE

CONDITION	TAKE-OFF	DIVING	LANDING	CRASH LANDING	LEVEL FLIGHT
Valve Position	Right or Reserve	Right or Reserve	Reserve	*Off	Left or Right

*Turn Valve "OFF" Immediately Before Ignition Switch is cut

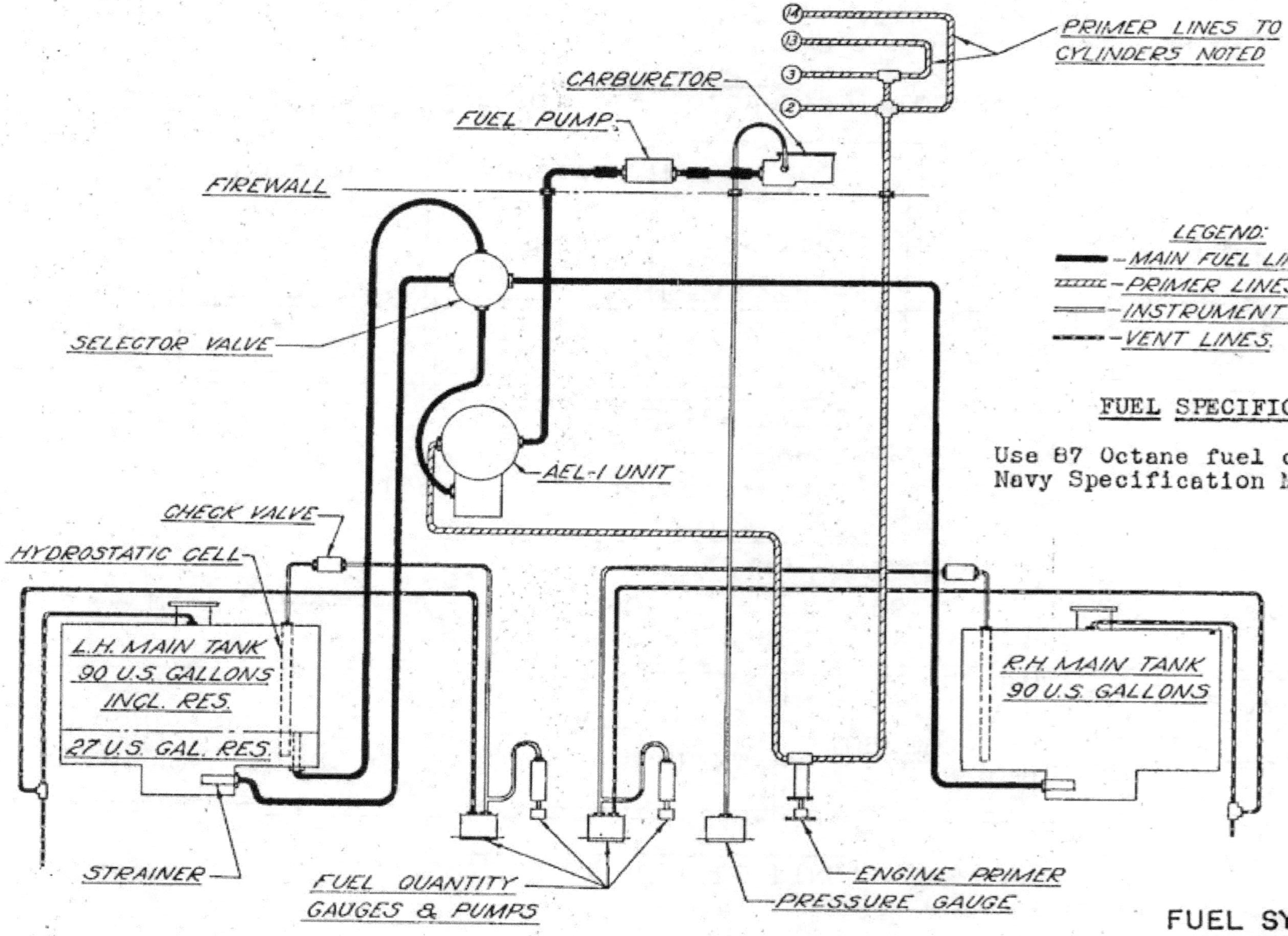

FUEL SPECIFICATION

Use 87 Octane fuel conforming to Navy Specification M-222 or M-302

FUEL SYSTEM
DIAGRAM

climb.

3. <u>Fuel Quantity Gauges</u>

a. This airplane is equipped with
MK. I hydrostatic type fuel quantity gauges,
one for each tank. Two positions are provided for: the three point attitude at
which time the thrust line is at an angle
of 13 3/4° and level flight at 132 knots
wherein the thrust line is at $+2^o$ to the
flight path. A calibration table is installed above the gauges and is to be used
to correct the gauge reading for the three
point attitude.

b. <u>Quantity Reading in Flight</u>

(1) Fly airplane at 132 knots in
steady level flight holding a constant
course.

(2) Pull plunger (L.H. or R.H.)
out and release allowing plunger to return
of its own accord.

(3) Repeat "(2)" one or more times.
<u>NOTE</u>: NO DEVIATION FROM FLIGHT
PATH ALLOWED FOLLOWING OPERATION OF PUMP
AND UNTIL GAUGE IS READ.

(4) Wait until pointer ceases to
fluctuate and take reading. (Reading must
be taken within one minute following operation of pump.

(5) Reading gives fuel quantity
for this condition.

c. <u>Quantity Reading - Three Point</u>

(1) Proceed as indicated in Paragraph "(2)" to "(5)" incl. under "b" preceding, except in "(5)", use conversion
table for correct quantity.

4. <u>Fuel Pressure</u>

a. Normally, the engine driven pump supplies fuel to the carburetor. For starting and in an emergency because of fuel pump failure, the wobble pump is operated to supply the necessary pressure. The following table shows fuel pressures for several conditions:

TABLE OF FUEL PRESSURES

Condition	Max	Min	Desired
Preparatory to starting		*2#	
Idling (400 r.p.m. or below)		2#	
Operation (above 1200 r.p.m.)	6#	4#	5#

*Build up with wobble pump

5. <u>Primer</u>

a. A priming system is used to facilitate engine starting. The primer draws fuel from the wobble pump and forces it directly to the cylinders where it enters in voltatile form as a spray.

b. It is recommended that when using the primer, the plunger be pulled out slowly to completely fill the cylinder and pushed in <u>rapidly</u> for a more even distribution and better vaporization.

c. Several strokes of the primer are required. The number of strokes varies with

(Oil System -
Tank, Temp. Cont.)

the temperature of the engine. Complete
data is given under instructions for starting the engine.

H. <u>Oil System</u>

   1. <u>Tank</u>

     a. The oil tank is installed forward
of the firewall in the engine section. The
tank is filled through an opening in the
cowling. The capacity of the tank is 12
gallons with an additional 3 gallons provided for foaming. A gauge stick on the
tank indicates the degree of fullness.

     b. The quantity of oil to be carried
varies with the type of armament installed
on the airplane. The following table indicates the amount of oil to be carried.

   2. <u>Temperature Control</u>

     a. Oil temperature control is auto-
matic and requires no attention from the
pilot. The oil <u>temperature regulator</u>
causes the oil to be brought up to proper
operating temperature rapidly and prevents
its over-cooling when operating at low
strut temperatures. The <u>oil cooler</u> prevents the oil from overheating.

     b. It is important that the oil tem-
perature be allowed to reach the required
minimum before the engine is revved up during warming. In very cold (sub-zero)
weather, an oil heater should be used prior
to starting the engine. Refer to the table
of oil temperatures and pressures, Page

(Oil Load., Temp., Pres.)

TABLE OF OIL LOADING

ARMAMENT LOADING CONDITION	SMOKE SCREEN LAYER	TORPEDO	BOMBER	
			3-500#	2-500# 1-1000# 12-100#
Gallons of Oil Carried	12	8*	10*	12

TABLE OF OIL TEMPERATURES AND PRESSURES

OPERATING CONDITION	OIL INLET TEMP. (°C.)			OIL PRESSURE (#/sq.in.)		
	Max.	Min.	Desired	Max.	Min.	Desired
Warm-up (before revving for flash run)		30		40		30
Warm-up (flash run)	70	40	65			90
Idling					15	
Take-Off	80	40	65	90	70	80
Cruising	80	40	65	90	50	80

*Normal oil load. Capacity load allowed with flight restrictions. See Page 76 .

(Oil System -
Pressure, Chk. Valve)

3. <u>Oil Pressure</u>

a. Oil pressure is a function of oil
temperature. When starting a cold engine,
the initial oil pressure is relatively high.
This is due to the fact that the oil is
cold, and, therefore, heavier than at normal
operating temperature. It requires more
pressure to force this heavy oil through the
system, hence the higher indicated oil pressure.

b. The table of oil temperatures and
pressures gives the allowable oil pressures
for various conditions of operation.

4. <u>A Check Valve</u> is incorporated within
the regulator unit which prevents oil from
the tank flowing back into the engine when
it is stopped.

I. <u>Carburetor Air Heat Control</u>

1. <u>Induction System</u>

a. Carburetor air is induced through
a duct having its opening in the form of
an air scoop on the R.H. side of the engine
section cowling. The scoop inlet provides
cold air. Below the scoop inlet and directly behind the exhaust stack, a second inlet in the duct provides for hot air. A
flap valve is used to completely close
either inlet, or it may be adjusted to any
intermediate position to vary the ratio of
hot and cold air.
b. The flap valve is controlled by
turning the knob on the instrument panel.

(Carb. Air Heat Cont. -
Induct. Sys., Air Temp.)

This reduction unit employs a worm and gear
so that the flap valve is locked in position
at all times. This provides a fine adjustment.

    c. <u>A Hot Spot</u> is installed on the
airplane but it is not connected when the
airplane leaves the factory. Therefore,
the use of carburetor air heat is important.

    2. <u>Air Temperatures</u>

    a. A thermometer bulb is installed in
the air duct immediately below the carburetor. The indicator is on the instrument
panel to the left of the heat control knob.

    b. Carburetor heat is provided for
two reasons: to better vaporize the fuel and
to prevent or eliminate carburetor icing.

    c. No heat should be used during take-
off unless the possibility of carburetor
icing (high humidity) is evident.

    d. It is recommended that following
take-off, carburetor air temperature be
maintained at 32-35°C. During climbs and
descents, the heat control will have to be
reset frequently. Whenever the throttle
is adjusted, the heat control will, likewise, need attention.

    e. <u>Whenever carburetor heat is ap-
plied, it is necessary to advance the
throttle and adjust the mixture.</u> This
is true because, when applying heat, the
flap valve closes off the cold air scoop,
thus eliminating its effect of carburetor
ram. With reduced ram, the efficiency
of the engine drops; hence the throttle
must be advanced in order to hold a given rpm.

(Carb. Air Heat Cont. -
Carburetor Icing)

With added heat it is possible to operate on
a leaner mixture; hence, the mixture control
is adjusted.

f. <u>Maximum available carburetor air
temperature can be raised 5° to 10°C.</u> by
changing the mixture from full rich to cor-
rect setting when heat is applied to the carburetor. This is true because a lean mixture
is less dense and consequently absorbs less
heat from the heating elements (air duct and
carburetor). With less heat consumed there
is more heat remaining to raise the air temperature. Also, the operating temperature
of the engine increases with leaned mixture.
Therefore, there will be hotter exhaust gas
available to heat the carburetor air, thus
raising it 5° to 10°C.

3. <u>Carburetor Icing</u>

a. The carburetor and induction system
as installed on this airplane is very suscep-
tible to icing. The pilot should, therefore, check the strut temperature indicator
at frequent intervals so that he may be in-
stantly aware of the probability of carburetor icing and adjust his heat accordingly.
It is desirable to prevent icing by the timely
use of heat. Once icing has occurred, more
heat will be required to remove it than
would have been necessary to prevent its
forming.

b. Carburetor icing may be expected
when flying in an area of high humidity with
strut temperatures from 0° to 30°C. if the
carburetor air temperature (gauge) is not
maintained at 32° to 35°C. A rich mixture
is more conducive to icing than a lean one.

(Carb. Air Heat Cont. -
Heat at Take-Off)

Icing may be detected at cruising throttle
settings by a gradual decrease in the manifold pressure at a fixed throttle setting
under steady flight (constant altitudes)
conditions. At throttle settings in excess
of 70% power it is more difficult to detect
except for irregular engine operation.
Test for icing as follows:

(1) Apply carburetor heat until
indicator shows 32°C.

(2) Hold "ON" for fifteen to
twenty seconds, then turn to full "COLD".

(3) If ice exists in the carburetor, the manifold pressure will increase
with the application of heat.

c. When it is evident that carburetor
icing has occurred, apply heat <u>full on</u> until temperature reaches 35°C. At this point
shut off heat gradually to maintain temperature between 32° to 35°C. Do not use
carburetor heat spasmodically. Keep the
heater on constantly rather than attempt to
melt the ice out periodically. Applying
heat periodically causes uneven engine
operation, loss of power and high fuel consumption.

4. <u>Heat at Take-Off</u>

a. It is recommended that <u>no</u> carburetor air heat be used for take-off unless
necessary to prevent carburetor icing.
With the use of heat there results a definite drop in power output caused by a
decrease in the density of the incoming
charge. This condition is not critical,
however, for ordinary take-off operations.

b. When icing conditions prevail at take-off, apply just sufficient heat (from one to three turns of control knob) to prevent ice formation in the carburetor.

5. Heat and Fuel Economy

a. When using carburetor heat, fuel consumption will increase because of enrichened mixture unless mixture is leaned out properly.

b. For maximum fuel economy with heat on, lean out mixture to allowable extent for the particular flight condition.

(Instrument Readings)

SECTION III

NORMAL INSTRUMENT READINGS

A. The table on the following page consists of observations and instrument readings as were recorded during a test flight. The airplane was loaded as shown below:

Item	Wt.
Airplane, as weighed	5573.0
Pilot and Chute	200.0
Observer and Chute	180.0
Fuel, 180 gal.	1080.0
Oil, 12 gal.	90.0
Rear 500# bomb	500.0
Ballast, Gunner's Seat	100.0
Gross Weight	7723.0
C.G. Location	26.41% M. A. C.

TABLE OF NORMAL CONDITIONS
AND INSTRUMENT READINGS

ITEM	TAKE-OFF	CRUISING
Cowl Flaps	Partly Closed	Closed
Mixture	Full Rich	Best Power
Carb. Air Temp. Cont.	Cold	Cold
Propeller Pitch	Low	High
Manifold Pressure	37"	27"
R.P.M.	2500	2100
Eng. Power Output	Full	65%
Altitude		4000'
Airspeed-Indicated		143 knots
Strut Temperature	25°C	12°C
Oil Pressure	85#	75#
Oil Temperature	65°C	65°C
Fuel Pressure	5#	5#
Carburetor Air Temp.	25°C	15°C
Cylinder Head Temp.	230°C	200°C
Take-Off Run (approx.)	980' Bomb or Torp	
Wind Conditions	0-1 knot	
Take-Off Time	17.3 sec.	
Wing Flaps	0°	0°
Aileron Tab	0°	0°
Elevator Tab	3° up	0°
Rudder Tab	3°R	3°R
Fuel Consumption		45.6 GPH

(Flying Char.-
Balance)

SECTION IV

FLYING CHARACTERISTICS

A. Balance

1. The position of the C.G. in terms of
percent (%) M.A.C. will vary according to
the loading condition of the airplane. Normal
flight and landing conditions exist between
20% to 30% M.A.C. With the C.G. forward of
the 20% position, the airplane is nose
heavy. When this condition exists, the
pilot should be aware of it so that he may
use caution in landing. It is recommended
that the pilot check the loading condition
of the airplane before takeoff so that he
may know what to expect in the way of flight
characteristics or "feel". Detailed information on balance is included in the "Handbook of Erection and Maintenance Instructions" furnished with this airplane.

2. When the airplane is ferried from the
factory, it is without armament and communicating equipment, and the pilot in the forward cockpit is the sole occupant. With
this set-up, the airplane is nose heavy.
To counteract this condition, a ballast
assembly weighing 500# complete, is installed on the aft bomb rack.

3. No ballast is required when the airplane is equipped complete for any one of
its several (torpedo, bomber, etc.) flight
conditions.

4. The probable necessity of ballast will arise when a flight is to be made without complete crew or equipment. The actual necessity and amount of ballast is determined by the use of the Loading Chart in the "Handbook of Erection and Maintenance Instructions".

B. Take-Off and Initial Climb

1. Use of Flaps in Take-Off

a. The use of flaps in take-off is dependent upon several variables: the gross weight of the airplane, length of the runway and whether or not there are obstructions to clear at the end of the runway. With the flaps lowered, the take-off run is shortened but the initial rate of climb is less than without flaps (See paragraph B, page 84). The effect of flaps on take-off run may be determined from the curves on page 82, while the diagram below gives a relative comparison.

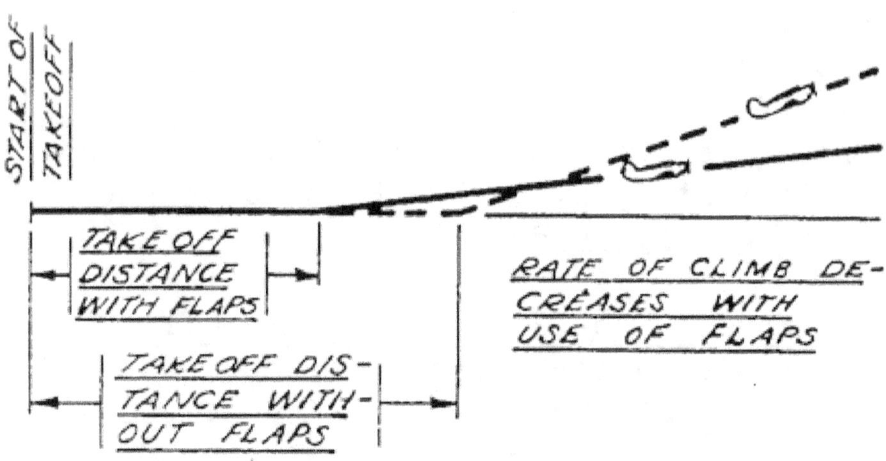

b. Carrier Take-Off's should be made with the flaps lowered 15°. Drop the flaps when the airplane is properly aligned at the

head of the runway. Taxiing with flaps
down is not recommended. Retract the
flaps when clear of the carrier and definite climb is established. A change of
trim will be noticed.

    c. <u>Short Field Take-Off's</u>

      (1) Where there are no obstruc-
tions to clear at the end of a short runway, a condition prevails similar to the
carrier take-off. See paragraph "b", preceding.

      (2) Where an obstruction (trees,
power line, etc.) occurs at the end of a
relatively short runway, it is recommended
that no flap be used. In this way, although the take-off run is extended, sufficient velocity is gained so that the
airplane will climb rapidly as it approaches
the obstruction, and will, in fact, clear
it by a wider margin than if flaps were
used. See diagram preceding.

    2. Whenever the airplane is heavily
loaded (9000#-10000#) or the take-off run
is limited, the pilot should check the
approximate take-off distance required as
may be determined from the curves, pages
79-84   . In general, the take-off
characteristics are normal. Rate of climb
is satisfactory even though the airplane
may be heavily loaded.

    3. <u>Rudder Tab Setting for Take-Off</u>

    a. It is important that the rudder
tab be properly set as this will aid considerably in holding a straight course
during the period of initial acceleration.

    b. Because of the variation in the

amount of rudder used between the start of the take-off and the time the airplane leaves the runway, the rudder tab setting must be a compromise. A setting of 3° RIGHT is recommended. With the tab in this position, the rudder is in good balance during the period of initial acceleration (a critical time in reference to ground-looping) and the airplane is more easily controlled. During the latter part of the take-off and in climbing, it will be necessary to use some right rudder.

4. <u>Take-Off "Check Off List"</u>

    a. Check of Airplane
       (1) Check all armament installations for security of mounting.
       (2) Check the airplane for proper balance.
    b. Check of Controls
       (1) Fuel on <u>RIGHT</u> or <u>RESERVE</u> tank.
    *(2) Propeller in <u>LOW</u> pitch.
    *(3) Cowl flaps <u>CLOSED</u>.
       (4) Tail wheel <u>LOCKED</u> (when in position for take-off).
    *(5) Carburetor air
       (a) Normally full <u>COLD</u>.
       (b) Icing possibilities - 1 to 3 turns of control knob.
    *(6) Mixture full <u>RICH</u>.
    *(7) Wing flaps 0° to 15°.
    *(8) Wings <u>SPREAD</u> and <u>LOCKED</u> (Indicator flag down and yellow).
       (9) Trim tabs
       (a) Aileron - 0°
       (b) Elevator - 0° to 3° nose up.
    *(c) Rudder - 3° <u>RIGHT</u>.

(Flying Char. -
Chk. of Eng., Execution)

NOTE: Additional experience in service may indicate better tab settings.

*More detailed information to be found as follows:

Item	Page	Paragraphs
(2)	41	1,2
(3)	39	D,E
(5)	52	4
(6)	37	C
(7)	57	1
(8)	20	1
(9)-(c)	75	C

c. Check of Engine
(1) Warm engine in preparation for flash run (See Page 33).
(2) Rev engine opening throttle to 30" Hg. Hold for about 10 seconds checking following:
(a) Oil pressure - 70-90#.
(b) Oil temperature above 40°C.
(c) R.P.M. (Sea Level) at 30" Hg. in low pitch, approximately 2200.
(d) Cylinder head temperatures - 150-200°C. (not to exceed 260°C).
d. Execution (Maximum Performance)
(1) Advance the throttle steadily to 37" manifold pressure allowing the airplane to roll and gain headway as the engine is accelerated.
(2) Raise the tail when it is ready to come up with normal pressure. Forcing it off with the elevators slows up the take-off because of excess drag from the depressed elevators.
(3) When the possibility of land-

MAXIMUM ALLOWABLE POWER OPERATION

Condition	Max. Man. Pressure	Max. RPM	Mixture Control	Prop. Setting
Take-Off, Sea Level (5 min. only)	37.0"	2500	Full Rich	Low
Climb to 3000'	34.5"	2450	Full Rich	Low
Level Flight, Sea Level - 3000'	34.5"	2450	Full Rich	High
Climb, 3000' - 6000'	33.5"	2450	Full Rich*	Low
Level Flight, 3000' - 6000'	33.5"	2450	Full Rich*	High
Climb, 6000' - 8000'	32.5"	2450	Smooth*** Engine	High** or Low
Level Flight, 6000' - 8000'	32.5"	2450	Smooth*** Engine	High
Operation Above 8000'	Unlimited	2450	Smooth*** Engine	High** or Low
Diving	37.0"	2950	Full Rich	High

*Lean only to maintain smooth engine operation above 4000'.

**Use "LOW PITCH" unless engine over-rev's (2450) at 32.5" Hg.

***Lean only enough to maintain smooth engine operation.

ing, should the need arise, is exceeded, retract the landing gear. (In carrier take-
off's, retract gear immediately after leav-
ing deck.)

(4) Close the throttle slowly until
the manifold pressure gauge reads 34.5" Hg.
Hold this pressure to 3000' altitude. The
recommended airspeed for climbing from sea
level to 8000' at 2450 r.p.m. in low pitch
is 85-90 knots.

(5) Under normal conditions allow
the indicated airspeed to increase to 85-90
knots. When the climb becomes steady at
this speed, retract the wing flaps (if they
were down). A change in trim will be noted.

(6) Continue climbing at 2450 r.p.m.
using manifold pressure as indicated and
watching engine temperatures.

Pressure Altitude			Manifold Pressure
Sea Level	to	3000'	34.5" Hg.
3000'	to	6000'	33.5" Hg.
6000'	to	8000'	32.5" Hg.

Maximum Cylinder Head Temp. - 260°C.
Maximum Oil Inlet Temperature - 85°C.

3. Take-Off Run vs. Altitude

a. The amount of time required and
the length of the take-off run increases
with an increase in altitude. The chart
on page 80 shows the effect of altitude
in take-off performance. These curves
are for "no flap" take-off. The curves
on page 82 show the effect of various degrees of flap.

(Flying Char. -
Level Flight, Cruis.)

C. High Speed Level Flight

1. Maximum performance in level flight is gained under the following operating conditions:

    a. Mixture - See page 38
    b. Propeller - High Pitch
    c. Manifold Pressure - As shown on page 62.
    d. Maximum R.P.M. - 2450
    e. Cowl Flaps - Use minimum opening necessary to hold cylinder head temperature to a continuous maximum of 260°C.
    f. Carburetor Air Temperature - Full Cold (or as required to prevent icing).

2. Under these conditions fuel consumption will be approximately 80 gallons per hour.

D. Cruising Operation

1. Cruising operation should not exceed 70% rated power. Maximum fuel economy is obtained below 70%.

2. For cruising operation, propeller is in HIGH pitch. R.P.M. and Manifold Pressure are determined from the cruising charts on pages 86-90. See tabulation on following page.

E. Maneuvers

1. This airplane can satisfactorily perform the following maneuvers:

MAXIMUM ALLOWABLE CONDITIONS FOR CONTINUOUS CRUISING OPERATION

ALTITUDE	MANIFOLD PRESS. "Hg.	R.P.M.	FUEL CONSUMP. Gal./Hr.	TRUE AIRSPEED KNOTS
Sea Level	A.--29.3" B.--29.5"	A.--2050 B.--2000	56	A.--149.5 B.--144
3000'	A.--28.0" B.--28.2"	A.--2100 B.--2060	56	A.--154 B.--148
6000'	A.--26.5" B.--27.0"	A.--2160 B.--2120	56	A.--158 B.--152
9000'	A.--25.5" B.--26.0"	A.--2210 B.--2175	57	A.--163 B.--156
12000'	A.--24.5" B.--25.0"	A.--2300 B.--2250	57	A.--167 B.--160
15000'	A.--23.5" B.--23.5"	A.--2350 B.--2300	57	A.--173 B.--164

1. This tabulation based on 70% rated power (600 BHP).
2. Mixture may be leaned to give drop of 20 R.P.M.
3. Propeller Setting - "HIGH PITCH".
4. Data marked: -   A. - Without Bombs or Torpedo.
                    B. - With Bombs or Torpedo.

(Flying Char. -
Maneuvers, Diving)

    a. Normal banks
    b. Spins - 1 1/2 turns
       (1) Flaps and gear up
       (2) Flaps and gear down
    c. Slips
       (1) Flaps and gear up
       (2) Flaps and gear down
    d. Dives to 206 knots
  *e. Pull outs to 4.8 g
    f. Wing overs
    g. Stalls
       (1) Flaps and gear up
       (2) Flaps and gear down

*NOTE: The airplane is designed for a normal pull out load of ≠ 4 and -2 g at 9300# gross weight, and ≠3.52 and -1.76 g at 10176# gross weight.

These maneuvers were completed with the airplane loaded:

    a. As a bomber
       3-500# bombs - Weight 9131#-
M.A.C. 29.0%.
    b. Torpedo airplane
       MK XIII torpedo - Weight
9273# - M.A.C. 25.45%.

   2. Diving

2500 a. The maximum allowable r.p.m. is ~~2950~~. DO NOT EXCEED THIS LIMIT.
    b. Before diving, check the following:
       (1) Cowl flaps CLOSED.
       (2) Wing flaps UP.
       (3) Fuel on RIGHT or RESERVE.
       (4) Mixture FULL RICH.

(Flying Char. -
Diving)

(5) Propeller on <u>HIGH</u> pitch

(6) Carburetor heat <u>FULL ON</u> (for long dives and <u>ON</u> 4 to 6 turns for short dives.)

<u>NOTE</u>: In order to keep the engine running smoothly, overcooling must be prevented and the fuel spilled within the carburetor during the dive, must be burned. Opening the throttle a small amount during the dive will accomplish this.

c. Pull outs are limited to 4 g at 9300# (normal gross weight) and 3.52 g at 10176# (maximum allowable gross weight).

SECTION V

LANDING CHARACTERISTICS

A. Use of Flaps in Landing

1. The wing flaps should be used for all landings because of the resultant decrease in landing speed. The stalling speed of the airplane at the normal gross weight (9300#) without the use of flaps is 66 knots as compared to 58 knots with the flaps down.

2. Before lowering the flaps, the airspeed should be reduced to 95 knots. As an aid in slowing the airplane, lower the landing gear first. NOTE: Such maneuvers as side slipping to reduce speed in a steep glide are not necessary nor are they desirable.

3. Overshooting - In case of overshooting a landing proceed as follows:

    a. Leave the flaps down.
    b. Open the throttle to 34.5 - 37" Hg. manifold pressure.
    c. Hold airspeed at 85-90 knots.
    d. Watch cylinder head temperature. Maximum allowable is $290^{\circ}C$. Open cowl flaps as necessary.
    e. Carburetor air heat OFF or as necessary to prevent icing.
    d. When at safe altitude, level off and raise flaps.

(Landing Char. -
Emer. Land. on Water)

4. Wind Conditions

If flaps are used in a relatively high
wind, it will be found easier to keep the
airplane on the runway after landing if the
pilot raises the flaps as soon as possible
after landing. This procedure "spills" the
lifting force from the flaps and prevents
the plane from being lifted off the runway.

5. Muddy Field Landings

When landing on wet or muddy fields,
raise the flaps as soon as possible after
the wheels touch the ground. In this way
the flaps will not be subjected to possible
damage through splashing of mud and rocks.

B. Emergency Landing On Water

1. When it is evident that it will be
necessary to alight on water, proceed as
follows:

    a. Clear all bomb and torpedo racks
(drop unarmed) by pulling emergency bomb
and torpedo release lever.
    b. Check position of wheels:
      (1) Wheels UP - recommended
      (2) NOTE: Best position for wheels
doubtful. Until further experience is
gained, no specific instructions can be is-
sued.
    c. Extend flaps (DOWN).
    d. Adjust pilot's and gunner's seats
to lowest positions.
    e. Open cockpit enclosures.

f. Stow or secure all movable pieces of equipment.

g. Set mixture full lean.

h. Set fuel tank selector to "OFF".

i. Cut ignition switch.

j. Cut main line battery and generator switches (gunner's cockpit).

k. Upon touching water, or as soon thereafter as possible, pull flotation gear release handle on shelf behind pilot's seat.

NOTE: The flotation gear is actuated automatically when a landing is made on water. However, the operation may be delayed somewhat over that of manual operation. Manual operation is recommended whenever possible.

C. Normal Landing - Sequence of Events

1. Descent

a. Before beginning the descent check aileron tab setting. Fly level at 130 knots and trim ailerons with tab. This setting is correct for descent, approach and landing.

NOTE: The fixed tab on the right aileron should be adjusted so that the airplane is properly trimmed (with symmetrical fuel and armament load) when the controllable tab is at neutral (0° setting) and when flying level at 130 knots indicated airspeed.

b. Nose airplane down and throttle back to about 95-100 knots at approximately 2100 r.p.m. in low pitch. Mixture Full Rich.

NOTE: Indicated airspeed does not change with altitude. Approach for landing at given airspeed, regardless of altitude.

    c. Re-balance airplane with elevator tabs.

    d. Cowl flaps closed.

    e. Carburetor air heat ON as little as possible to hold temperature at 32-35°C.

    2. <u>Approach</u>

    a. Drop landing gear.
    b. Lower wing flaps.
    <u>NOTE</u>: FLAP WARNING - DO NOT BEGIN TO LOWER FLAPS ABOVE 110 KNOTS
    c. Re-balance airplane with elevator tabs. (Lowering flaps causes change in balance.)
    d. Close throttle (not fully) and set elevator tabs at 6°-12° nose up (depending on load carried).
    e. Check rudder tab - 3° RIGHT.
    f. Watch cylinder temperatures (above 150°C) and approach with some power on to prevent over-cooling and choking of the engine. Torching and fire in the collector ring sometimes occurs after landing from a short glide with power off.
    g. Watch tendency to undershoot due to steepened gliding angle.
    h. Check carburetor air temperature.
    (1) Use as little heat as possible (normally 0-3 turns) to insure against icing.

    (2) Should it be necessary to use full throttle because of overshooting a landing, and the heat control is on more than 3 turns, the carburetor air may become over-heated resulting in a loss in power output.

(Landing Char. -
Landing, Chk.Off List)

3. Landing

    a. PILOT SHALL INSURE THAT ARRESTING GEAR HANDLE IS <u>SECURELY LOCKED</u> IN THE "HOOK" DOWN" POSITION PRIOR TO LANDING ABOARD A CARRIER.

    b. In field landings after rolling a short distance with the tail fully down, apply the brakes gradually in order to shorten the landing roll. The brakes operate independently (L.H. and R.H.) and may, therefore, be used to aid in directional control.

    c. Following completion of the landing roll, OPEN cowl flaps, retract wing flaps, and unlock tail wheel before taxiing.

    d. A chart showing the effect of altitude on landing speed (ground speed) will be found on Page 93.

4. <u>Landing "Check-Off List"</u>

    a. Landing gear <u>DOWN</u>.
    b. Fuel on <u>RESERVE</u>.
    c. Propeller in <u>LOW</u> pitch.
    d. Cowl flaps <u>CLOSED</u>.
    e. Tail wheel <u>LOCKED</u>.
    f. Carburetor air heat ON as required (See Paragraph 2-h, preceding).
    g. Mixture <u>FULL RICH</u>.
    h. Wing flaps <u>FULL DOWN</u>.
    i. Rudder tab - 3° <u>RIGHT</u>.
    j. Elevator tabs $6-12^\circ$ nose up.

5. <u>After Landing "Check-Off List"</u>

    a. Open cowl flaps immediately after landing and before taxiing.

(Landing Char. -
Taxiing)

    b. Raise wing flaps.
    c. Unlock tail wheel.

6. <u>Taxiing</u>

a. The airplane handles normally and satisfactorily during taxiing operation.

b. When taxiing at relatively high speed, the tail wheel should be locked. Directional control is possible through independent use of the left and right brakes.

c. It is recommended that the wing flaps be up for all taxiing operation. With the flaps down in a strong head wind, the tail becomes very light requiring added caution on the part of the pilot.

D. <u>Emergency Landing Without Hyd. Pressure</u>

1. Should the hydraulic reservoir or its immediate supply lines be damaged in flight allowing the fluid to drain out, the landing gear and wing flaps could yet be operated. Air pressure, built up with the hand hydraulic pump, is used. Sufficient fluid will remain in the lines and struts to act as a seal preventing air leakage.

2. When preparing to land, first drop gear.

a. This is done in the usual manner using the hand pump as a pressure source.
b. Refer to Paragraph (f), Page 25.

3. Following lowering of the landing gear, extend the flaps.

(<u>Emergency</u> Landing)

    a. Lowering the flaps is done in the usual manner using the hand pump as the source of pressure.

    b. Refer to Paragraph (d), Page 10.

SECTION VI

SPECIAL PRECAUTIONS

A. Restricted Maneuvers

1. Maneuvers Restricted By Design

    a. Acrobatics
    b. Inverted flight
    c. Dives in excess of 45°, 205 knots
and 2950 r.p.m.
    d. Pull-out's in excess of 4 g at a
normal gross weight of 9300#.

2. Voluntary Maneuvers Normally Restricted

    *a. Prolonged stalls
    *b. Spins
    **c. Steep slips

    *NOTE: Prolonged stalls and spins
impose excessive aerodynamic forces on the
airplane structure due to buffeting which,
if voluntarily maintained for an appreciable
length of time, might result in local fail-
ures.
    **NOTE: In a steep slip, the ele-
vators become very ineffective resulting in
a tail heavy condition.

B. Cockpit Enclosures

1. In flight or while revving the engine
on the ground, the pilot's cockpit hood will
open rapidly when the winch is unlocked due

(Spec. Precautions)

to the increased air pressure.

2. The pilot should use due caution in operating the control so that the hood will not be thrown open rapidly, causing damage.

C. <u>Trim Tabs</u>

1. Before taking off or landing insure that the tabs are properly set. This is particularly important in the case of elevator and rudder tabs. The airplane is slightly nose heavy in landing with an improper elevator tab adjustment. Ground loops may result from an improperly set rudder tab.

2. Tab instructions are included in the "Check Off Lists", pages 59,71.

D. <u>Water Landings</u>

1. Do not pull the flotation gear operating handle until the airplane has touched the water. The effect of the inflated bags on the flight characteristics of the airplane would be critical.

E. <u>Airplane Balance</u>

1. Check the airplane balance whenever full crew and equipment are not carried. (Loading Chart in Maintenance Handbook.) Add ballast as required to properly balance airplane. <u>NOTE</u>: This airplane may be flown by the pilot only with no armament or communicating equipment and no ballast. However,

(Spec. Precautions)

due caution must be used in landing as the airplane is nose havy under these conditions. It is recommended that ballast be used.

2. Pilot should be aware of any abnormal balance condition so that he may use his controls to aid in compensating for this condition.

F. Provisional Overload - Restrictions

1. Throughout this handbook all weight, range and endurance figures, given in connection with the MK XIII Torpedo or the 3-500# bomb condition, are in consideration of a normal gross weight of 9300#.

2. In order to increase the effectiveness of the airplane while carrying a MK XIII Torpedo or 3-500# bombs, overloading (in excess of 9300# gross) is permissible whereby full fuel (180 gal.) and full oil (12 gal.) may be carried with flight restrictions. Maximum allowable gross weight is 10176#.

3. Overload Flight Restrictions

a. When overloaded, applied accelerations must be reduced. At 10176# gross, the acceleration loads are restricted to $+3.52$ g and $- 1.76$ g as compared to $+4$ g and -2 g at 9300# gross.

b. For further data on flight restrictions, including permissible weights for landing, refer to Technical Order No. superseding T.O. No. 78-37.

(Spec. Precautions)

G. Ground Loop - Prevention Of

1. To the majority of Naval Flying Personnel, the TBD-1 Airplane will, until further experience is gained, present a problem in orientation during take-off and landing. This is true because the TBD-1 is radically different from previous naval aircraft. The upper wing is absent as are the customary wires and brace struts of the bi-plane, which the pilot has previously learned to use as an aid in proper orientation.

2. Ground Looping may sometimes occur following a landing in which the pilot had difficulty in lining the airplane up properly during the final stages of the approach and at the time of contact. In taking off, difficulty may, likewise, be experienced if the pilot fails to properly align the airplane previous to opening the throttle.

3. Anti-Groundloop Suggestions

a. In approaching insure that the rudder tab is properly set. Rudder tab settings between the neutral and 1600 r.p.m. balance setting are recommended for power stall landings.

b. Complete the latter portion of the approach in good alignment with the field (or deck) so that the airplane will not be in a skid when making contact.

c. Acquire proper orientation before the landing contact and maintain it until

landing is completed. Proper orientation
will result from concentrated attention on
the part of the pilot and experience.

H. Ground Loop - Recovery From

1. It is important to realize and act
quickly when a groundloop has begun. This
is considerably more difficult at night
due to difficulty in taking bearings.

2. The following procedure is recommended
and is applicable to groundloops at take-
off or landing.

    a. Use full opposite rudder
    b. Cut throttle
    c. Hold tail down
    d. Apply brakes easily keeping tail
on ground.

NOTE: The first 20°-30° of the loop
represents a period wherein, with the use
of full throttle (37" Hg.), the airplane
may be "hauled off". When this is reason-
ably possible, the pilot should resort to
this procedure. However, if the first
attempt is unsuccessful, use the procedure
recommended above.

I. Dropping of Torpedo

1. Serious structural damage may
result from dropping a torpedo while
flying too close to the surface. When
the torpedo strikes the water, a very
heavy spray is thrown up. DO NOT DROP
TORPEDO WITHIN 20 FEET OF THE SURFACE.

SECTION VII

OPERATION CHARTS AND CURVES

A. Take-Off Distance

1. Take-off distance will vary according to wind conditions, (field or carrier) altitude, temperature, weight of the airplane and the degree of flap used.

2. NO Flap Take-Off

a. For this condition, the curves on page 80 may be used directly to find take-off distance.

b. Examples Illustrating Use of Curves

(1) Carrier Take-Off (25 knot wind)

(a) Assuming the following conditions:

Atmospheric Temperature .... 25°C.
Gross Weight .... 9105#

it is desired to find the take-off distance required without the use of flaps.

(b) Refer to the curves for "no flap" take-off on page 80 and proceed as follows:

(c) Enter the chart at "S.L." on the altitude scale in the upper left hand corner.

(d) Move horizontally to a point corresponding to 25°C. (Point A).

(e) Drop vertically to a position corresponding to a weight of 9105# (Point B).

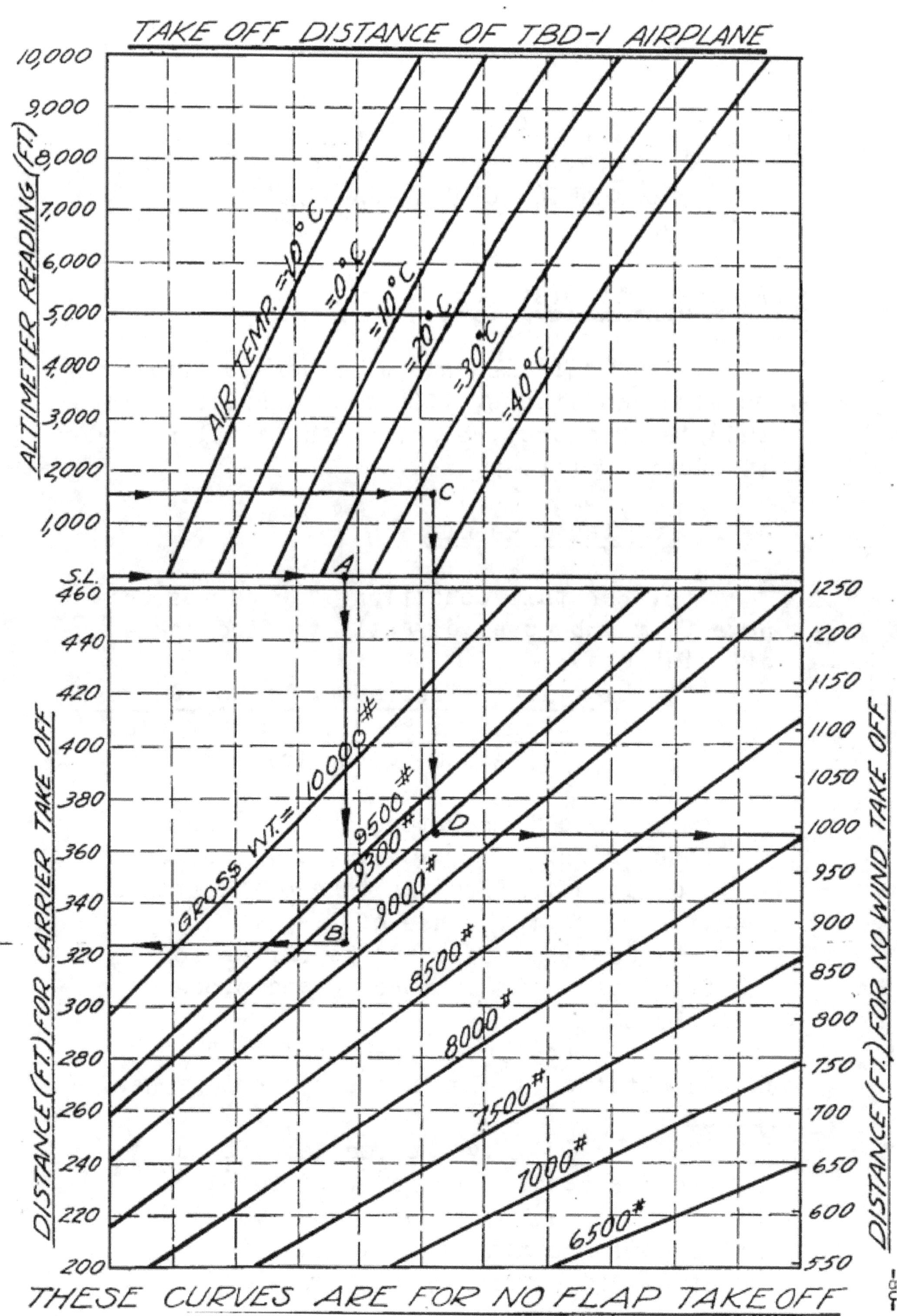

TAKE OFF DISTANCE OF TBD-1 AIRPLANE
ALTIMETER READING (FT.)
10,000
9,000
8,000
7,000
6,000
5,000
4,000
3,000
2,000
1,000
S.L.
AIR TEMP. =10°C
=0°C
=10°C
=20°C
=30°C
=40°C
C
A
DISTANCE (FT.) FOR CARRIER TAKE OFF
460
440
420
400
380
360
340
320
300
280
260
240
220
200
GROSS WT.= 10000#
9500#
9300#
9000#
8500#
8000#
7500#
7000#
6500#
B
D
DISTANCE (FT.) FOR NO WIND TAKE OFF
1250
1200
1150
1100
1050
1000
950
900
850
800
750
700
650
600
550
THESE CURVES ARE FOR NO FLAP TAKE OFF

(f) Move horizontally to the left, reading the desired distance on the vertical "carrier take-off" scale, <u>322 feet</u>.

(2) <u>Field Take-Off</u> (no wind)

(a) Assuming the following conditions exist:

Altitude .... 1500'
Atmospheric Temperature .... 33°C.
Gross Weight .... 9289#

it is desired to find the take-off distance required without the use of flaps.

(b) Refer to the curves for "no flap" take-off, page 80 and proceed as follows:

(c) Enter the chart at 1500' on the scale in the upper left hand corner.

(d) Go horizontally to a point corresponding to 33°C. (Point C).

(e) Drop vertically to a point indicative of 9289# (Point D).

(f) Move horizontally to the right reading the desired distance on the "no wind take-off" scale, <u>992 feet</u>.

3. <u>Effect of Flaps on Take-Off Distance</u>

a. With the use of flaps the take-off distance is shortened. This distance continues to decrease with additional degrees of flap. See page 82 . However, the rate of climb falls appreciably so that a flap depression in excess of 20° is seldom used although take-off may be accomplished with full flap depression (45°).

b. The curves, page 82 , show the percent reduction in take-off distance vs. flap angle for standard carrier take-off's (curves B to G incl.) and for no wind take-off (Curve A). The latter curve is

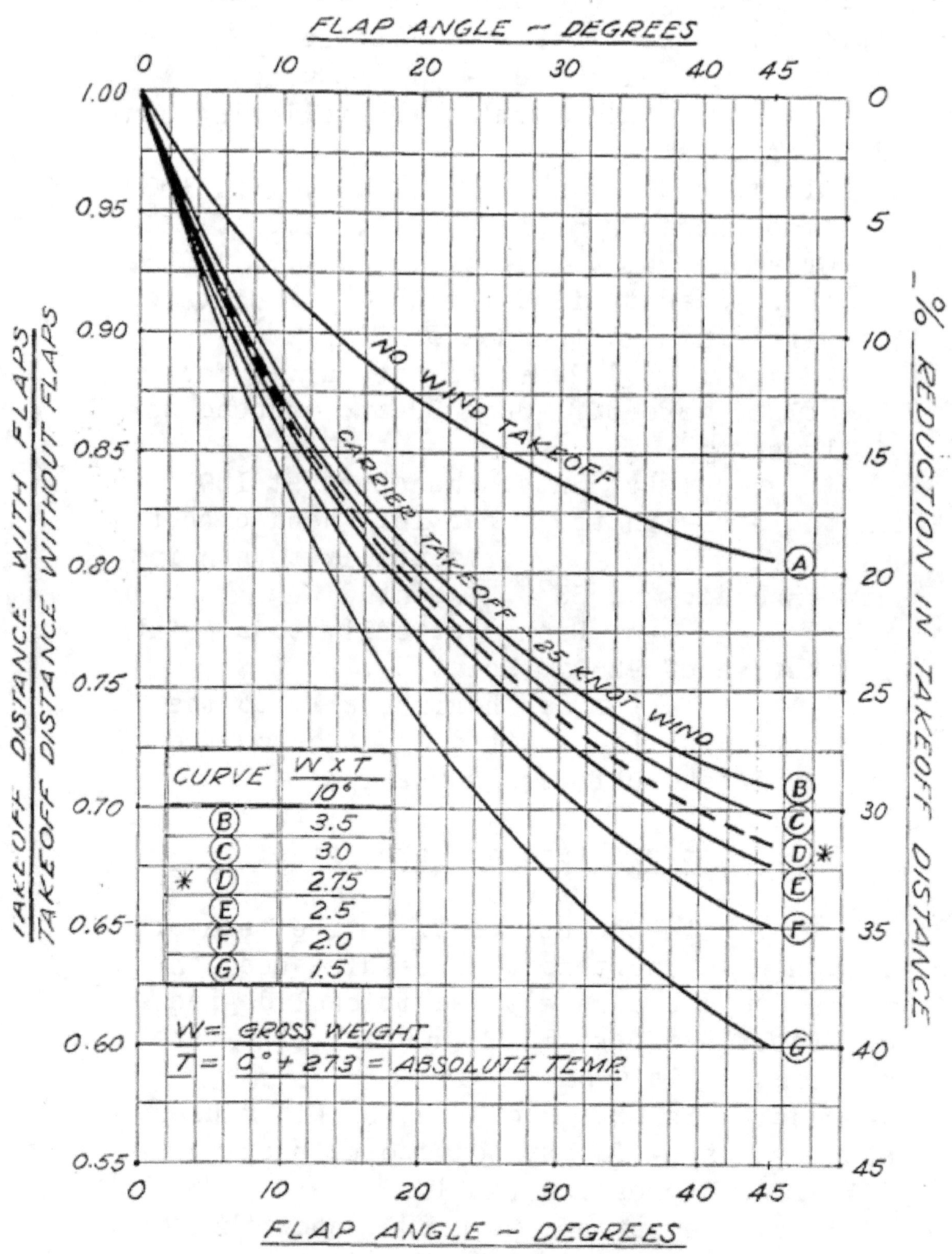

CURVES SHOWING EFFECT OF FLAPS
ON TAKEOFF DISTANCE
FLAP ANGLE ~ DEGREES
0   10   20   30   40   45
- % REDUCTION IN TAKEOFF DISTANCE
TAKEOFF DISTANCE WITH FLAPS / TAKEOFF DISTANCE WITHOUT FLAPS
NO WIND TAKEOFF
CARRIER TAKEOFF - 25 KNOT WIND
A
B
C
D *
E
F
G
CURVE   W X T / 10^6
B   3.5
C   3.0
* D   2.75
E   2.5
F   2.0
G   1.5
W = GROSS WEIGHT
T = C° + 273 = ABSOLUTE TEMP.
FLAP ANGLE ~ DEGREES
* DOTTED CURVE REPRESENTS TAKEOFF AT
STD. SEA LEVEL TEMP. (15°C + 273 = 288° ABS.)
WITH 9300# GROSS WEIGHT

almost entirely a function of maximum lift
co-efficient and, therefore, is independent
of weight, altitude and temperature. Flap
effect in carrier take-off depends upon the
relation of take-off velocity to the wind
velocity (25 knots) as well as the change
in maximum lift co-efficient. For this
reason flap effect must be plotted for a
series of values of W x T, (gross weight) x
(absolute temperature). Each curve (B to G
incl.) in the carrier take-off group represents a separate value of W x T. For convenience these values are divided by 10^6 and
tabulated below the curves. The dotted
curve is included for convenience and represents take-off at standard sea level conditions at a normal gross weight of 9300#.
These curves serve a dual purpose as two
quantities may be found. The required flap
depression for a known take-off run or the
effect of a given flap depression or take-
off run may be determined.

    c. <u>Examples Illustrating Use of Curves</u>
       (1) <u>Field Take-Off (no wind)</u>
        (a) Having previously determined
the "no flap take-off" distance (992') as
shown in paragraph (2), page 81, it is desired to know the amount of flap depression
(degrees) necessary to reduce the take-off
distance by 100' (approximately 10%).

        (b) Turning to the curves on
page 82, choose a point on the "no wind
take-off" curve (A), equivalent to 10% as
indicated by the vertical scale on the right.

        (c) This point is then found to
be equivalent to 11.7° of flap angle as indicated on the horizontal scale.

        (d) Summarizing the results, we
find that, at 1500' (no wind) at 33°C. with a

gross weight of 9289#, requiring a run of 992' for no flaps, in order to reduce the run by 100', it will be necessary to use 11.7° flap depression.

(2) <u>Carrier Take-Off</u> (25 knot wind)

(a) Having previously determined the "no flap take-off" distance (332') as shown in paragraph (1), page 81, it is desired to know the amount of flap depression necessary to reduce the take-off run 60' (approximately 18 1/2%).

(b) Turning to the curves on page 82 , we find it first necessary to determine the value of $\underline{W \times T}$. From the original assumptions, 10^6 (paragraph (1), page 79), the weight is 9105# and the temperature 25°C., thus:

$$\frac{9105 \times (25° + 273)}{10^6} = 2.71$$

(c) From the tabulation below the curves we find that Curve D approximates our value of 2.71.

(d) On curve D, locate a point equivalent to 18 1/2% as shown by the vertical scale on the left.

(e) Comparing this point on the curve with the horizontal scale, we find that 16° flap depression must be used.

(f) Summarizing the results, we find that for carrier take-off with 9105# gross weight at 25°C. requiring a run of 322' for "no flap take-off", in order to reduce this run by 60', it will be necessary to use 16° of flap.

B. Effect of Flaps on Angle of Climb at Take-Off

1. The problem of flap use at take-off

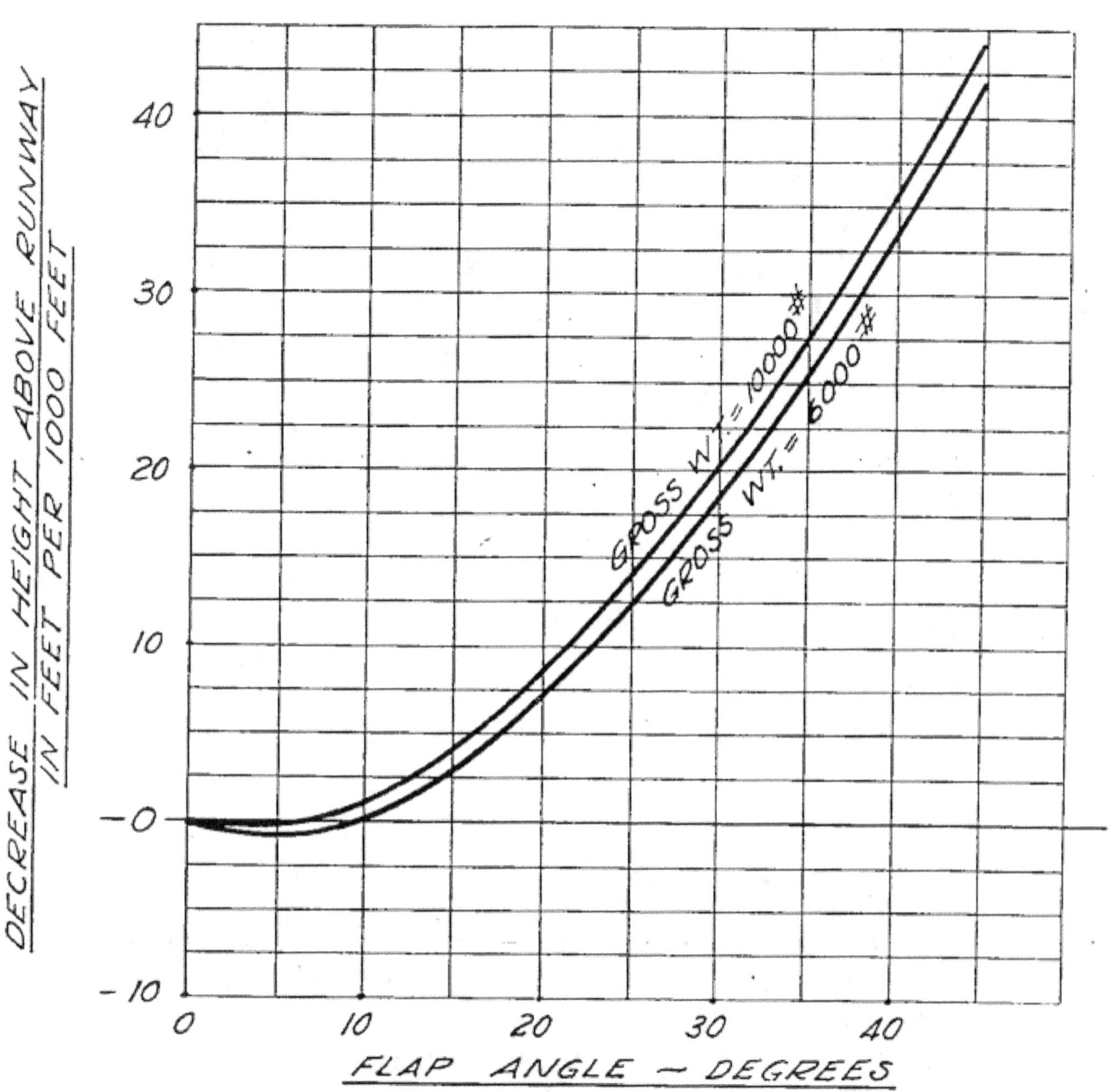

EFFECT OF FLAPS
ON ANGLE OF CLIMB
AT TAKEOFF
DECREASE IN HEIGHT ABOVE RUNWAY IN FEET PER 1000 FEET
40
30
20
10
-0
-10
0
10
20
30
40
FLAP ANGLE — DEGREES
GROSS WT. = 10000 #
GROSS WT. = 6000 #

(Take-Off - Angle of
Climb)

becomes extremely important in field operation where there is an obstacle to clear
at the end of a relatively short runway.
To compensate for the short runway, flaps
would ordinarily be used. However, the use
of flaps will handicap the effective climb.
The problem, therefore, is to use only
enough flap to clear both the end of the
runway and the obstacle.

2. The curves on page 85 show the decrease in height above the runway for each
1000' the airplane progresses horizontally
as compared to the angle of flap depression.
Two curves are plotted, one for a gross
weight of 6000# and one for 10000#. There
are no correction factors necessary in the
plotting of these curves. Therefore, simplicity is maintained and results may be
read off directly by determining gross
weight and flap angle. The scale on the
left is laid out to give obstacle clearances
directly rather than rate of climb as the
former is more convenient.

C. <u>Cruising Charts</u>

1. Two cruising charts are provided: one
for a gross weight of approximately 9000#,
comparable to the bomb or torpedo condition,
and the other for a gross weight of about
7600# which will approximate the condition
wherein no bombs or torpedo are carried.
The charts show the Power Output (in percent
rated power) R.P.M. and Manifold Pressure
necessary to maintain level flight at any
<u>true airspeed</u> at any altitude and tempera-
ture.

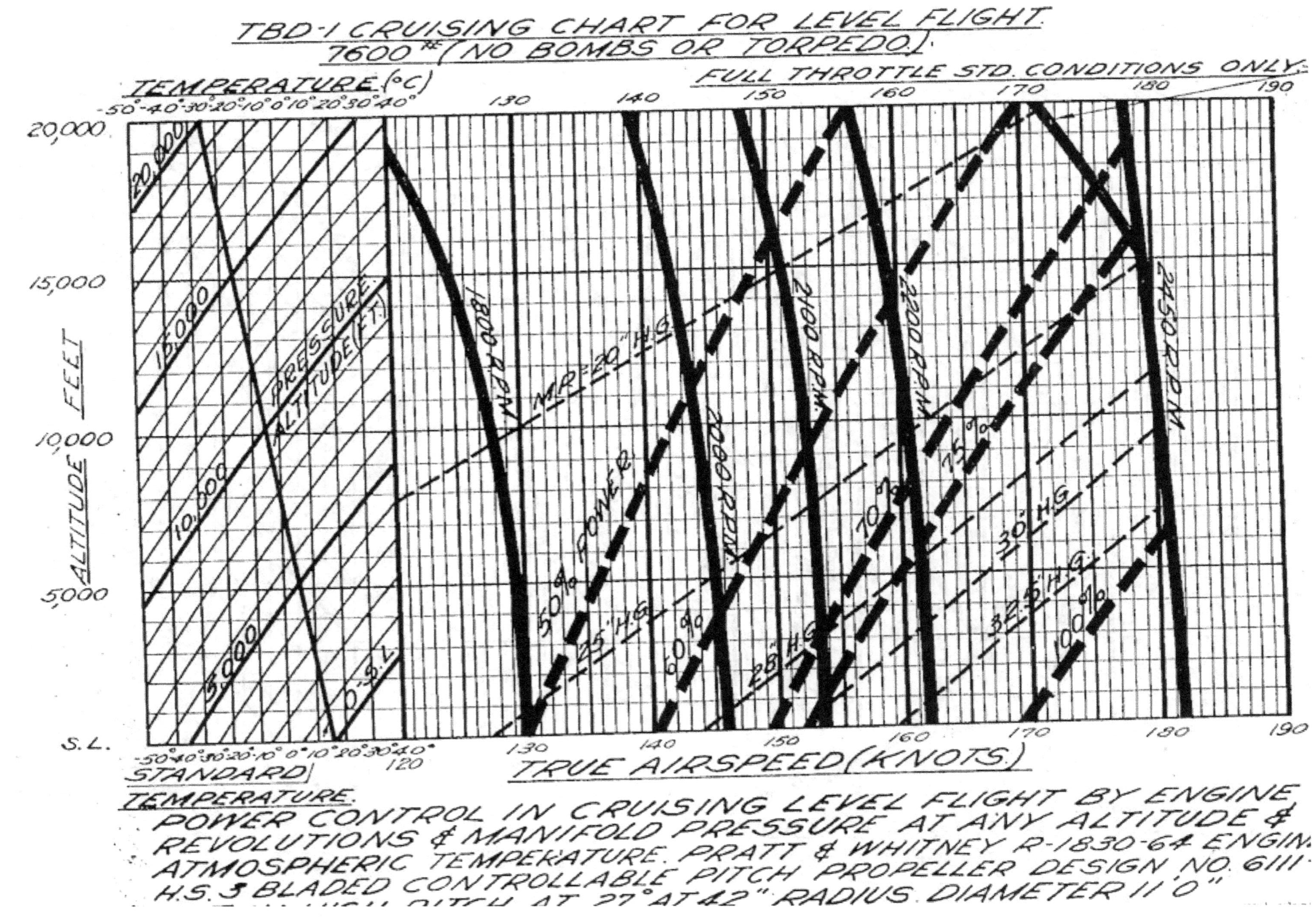

TBD-1 CRUISING CHART FOR LEVEL FLIGHT.
7600 # (NO BOMBS OR TORPEDO.)
FULL THROTTLE STD. CONDITIONS ONLY.
TEMPERATURE (°C)
-50° -40° -30° -20° -10° 0° 10° 20° 30° 40°
20,000
15,000
10,000
5,000
ALTITUDE FEET
PRESSURE ALTITUDE (FT)
20,000
15,000
10,000
5,000
S.L.
1800 R.P.M.
2000 R.P.M.
2100 R.P.M.
2200 R.P.M.
2450 R.P.M.
M.P.-20" H.G.
50% POWER
60%
70%
75%
100%
25" H.G.
28" H.G.
30" H.G.
32.5" H.G.
130 140 150 160 170 180 190
120 130 140 150 160 170 180 190
TRUE AIRSPEED (KNOTS.)
-50° -40° -30° -20° -10° 0° 10° 20° 30° 40°
STANDARD
TEMPERATURE.
POWER CONTROL IN CRUISING LEVEL FLIGHT BY ENGINE
REVOLUTIONS & MANIFOLD PRESSURE AT ANY ALTITUDE &
ATMOSPHERIC TEMPERATURE. PRATT & WHITNEY R-1830-64 ENGIN.
H.S. 3 BLADED CONTROLLABLE PITCH PROPELLER DESIGN NO. 6111.
HIGH PITCH AT 27° AT 42" RADIUS. DIAMETER 11'0"

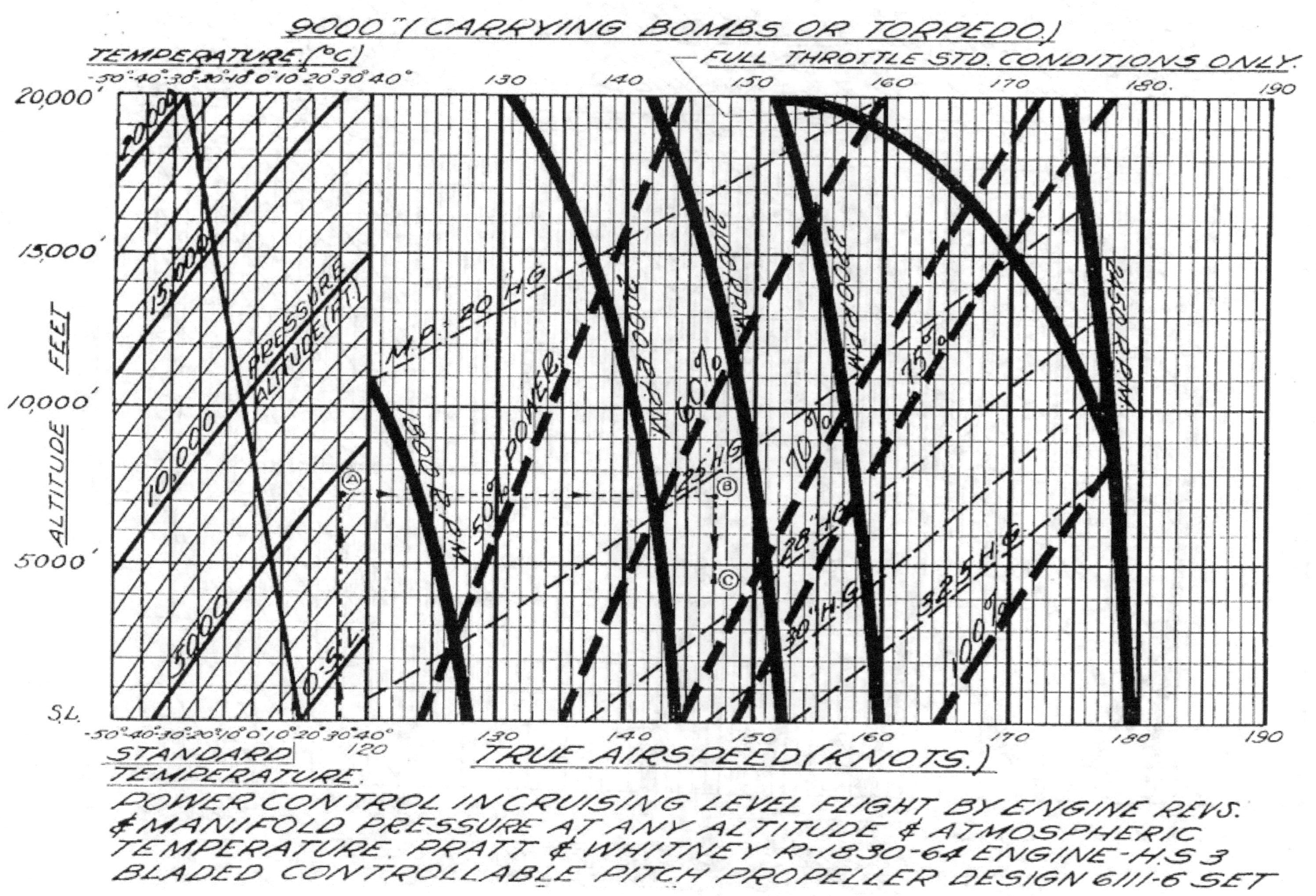

9000"/ (CARRYING BOMBS OR TORPEDO.)
FULL THROTTLE STD. CONDITIONS ONLY.
TEMPERATURE. (°C)
-50° -40° -30° -20° -10° 0° 10° 20° 30° 40°
20,000'
15,000'
10,000'
5000'
S.L.
ALTITUDE FEET
PRESSURE ALTITUDE (FT.)
20,000
15,000
10,000
5000
0 S.L.
130 140 150 160 170 180. 190
M.P. 20" HG
1800 R.P.M
50% POWER
1900 R.P.M.
2000 R.P.M.
2100 R.P.M.
2200 R.P.M.
2450 R.P.M.
60%
70%
75%
80%
90%
25" HG
28" HG
30" H.G.
32.5 HG
-50° -40° -30° -20° -10° 0° 10° 20° 30° 40°
120 130 140 150 160 170 180 190
STANDARD TEMPERATURE.
TRUE AIRSPEED (KNOTS.)
POWER CONTROL IN CRUISING LEVEL FLIGHT BY ENGINE REVS.
& MANIFOLD PRESSURE AT ANY ALTITUDE & ATMOSPHERIC
TEMPERATURE. PRATT & WHITNEY R-1830-64 ENGINE - H.S 3
BLADED CONTROLLABLE PITCH PROPELLER DESIGN 6111-6 SET

(Cruising Charts)

2. Since the Power Output and R.P.M. depend on density altitude, a small chart is included on the left of the sheet for deriving density altitude from pressure altitude (altimeter) and atmospheric (strut) temperature. The manifold pressure depends upon the pressure altitude (altimeter) reading.

3. <u>Example Illustrating Use of Chart</u>

a. Assuming the following conditions:
Loading condition .... 3-500# bombs
Altimeter reading .... 4500'
Atmospheric (strut) temp. ...... 30°C.
True airspeed .... 147 knots
it is desired to find the Power Output, R.P.M. and Manifold Pressure necessary to maintain level flight.
b. Refer to the chart for the 9000# condition on page 88 and proceed as follows:
(1) Enter the chart on the temperature scale at the lower left of the sheet at the 30°C. mark.
(2) Move vertically to a point corresponding to a pressure altitude (altimeter reading) of 4500' (Point A). This gives the correct density altitude, (approximately 7200').
(3) Go horizontally to a point corresponding to 147 knots (Point B). Here from the R.P.M. lines (heavy solid) we estimate 2060 r.p.m. and from the Percent Power lines (heavy dash) we estimate 63% power.
(4) To find Manifold Pressure, drop vertically to a point corresponding to an altitude of 4500' (Point C) as indicated by scale on extreme left. Here we estimate the manifold pressure (thin dash lines) to

be 27" Hg.

(5) Summarizing the results we find
that it is necessary to use 63% power at 2060
r.p.m. at 27" Hg. to maintain level flight
at 147 knots.

D. Fuel Consumption Curves

1. The fuel consumption chart furnished on
page 91 compares fuel mileage in nautical
miles per gallon with airspeed (indicator
reading). The chart can be used for two purposes: to find the required fuel load for a
given mission at a predetermined airspeed
(Example A) or to give the airspeed (indicated) for a given mission with a given amount
of fuel (Example B).

2. If true airspeed is desired rather than
indicated airspeed, or vice versa, use the
airspeed correction chart on page 95.

3. Examples Illustrating Use of Chart

a. To find amount of fuel
(1) Assuming the following:
"It is desired to carry a tor-
pedo 50 nautical miles at a true airspeed of
160 knots at 2000' (air temp. 25°C.), drop
the torpedo and return at the same speed and
altitude."
What fuel load (number of gallons) should be carried?
(2) From the airspeed correction
chart 160 knots true airspeed at 2000' at
25°C. is equivalent to an indicator reading
of 151 knots.

TABLE OF CONTENTS

FUEL CONSUMPTION CURVES

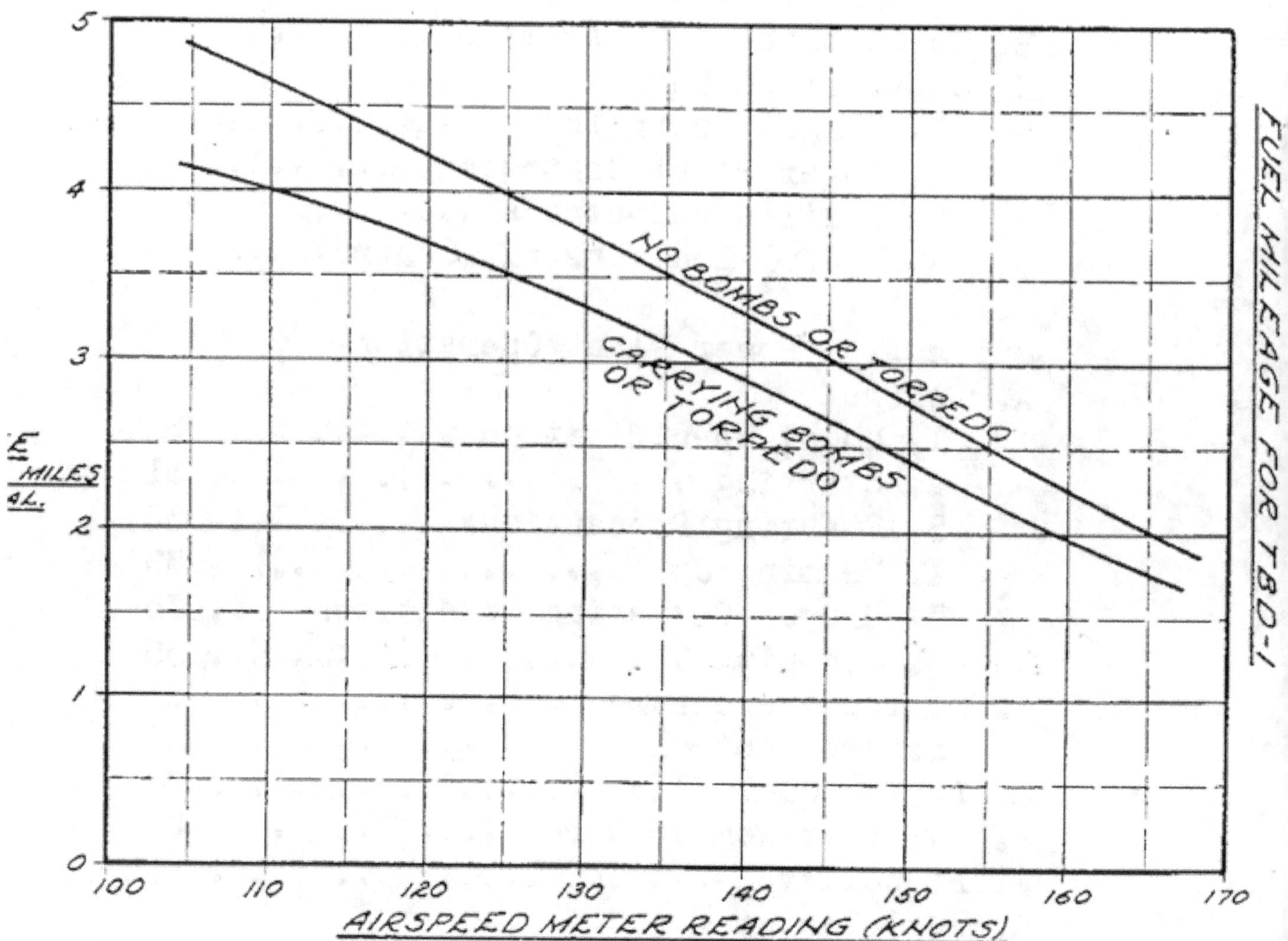

NOTE:— THESE CURVES ARE CONTINGENT UPON THE USE OF 87 OCTANE FUEL (NAVY SPECIFICATION M222 OR M302) AND THE PROPER OPERATION OF THE CARBURETOR MIXTURE CONTROL

(Landing Speed Curves)

(3) From the Fuel Consumption Chart, for torpedo condition, the mileage is 2.4. For the no load condition (return flight) the fuel mileage is 2.7.

(4) To find the gallons required:

$$\frac{50}{2.4} + \frac{50}{2.7} = 39.3 \text{ gallons}$$

Allowing 27 gallons reserve for take-off and landing we have:

$$39.3 + 27 = 66.3 \text{ gallons}$$

    b. To find airspeed:

(1) Assuming the following:

"It is desired to ferry the airplane (no bombs or torpedo) a distance of 300 nautical miles and arrive with a reserve of 40 gallons of fuel. The maximum fuel load is 180 gallons for this condition."

What is the maximum airspeed (indicated) possible?

(2) Usable fuel is 180 - 40 = 140 gallons.

(3) The least possible fuel mileage is $\frac{300}{140}$ = 2.14 nautical miles per gallon.

(4) From the chart we find that 2.14 n.m.p.g. allows an indicated airspeed of 161 knots.

E. <u>Landing Speed Curves</u>

1. The landing (or stalling) speed of the airplane in terms of Indicated Airspeed increases with an increase in weight and does not vary with altitude. Curve "B" of the chart on page 93 gives the stalling (indicated) airspeed with gross loads from 6000# to 10000#.

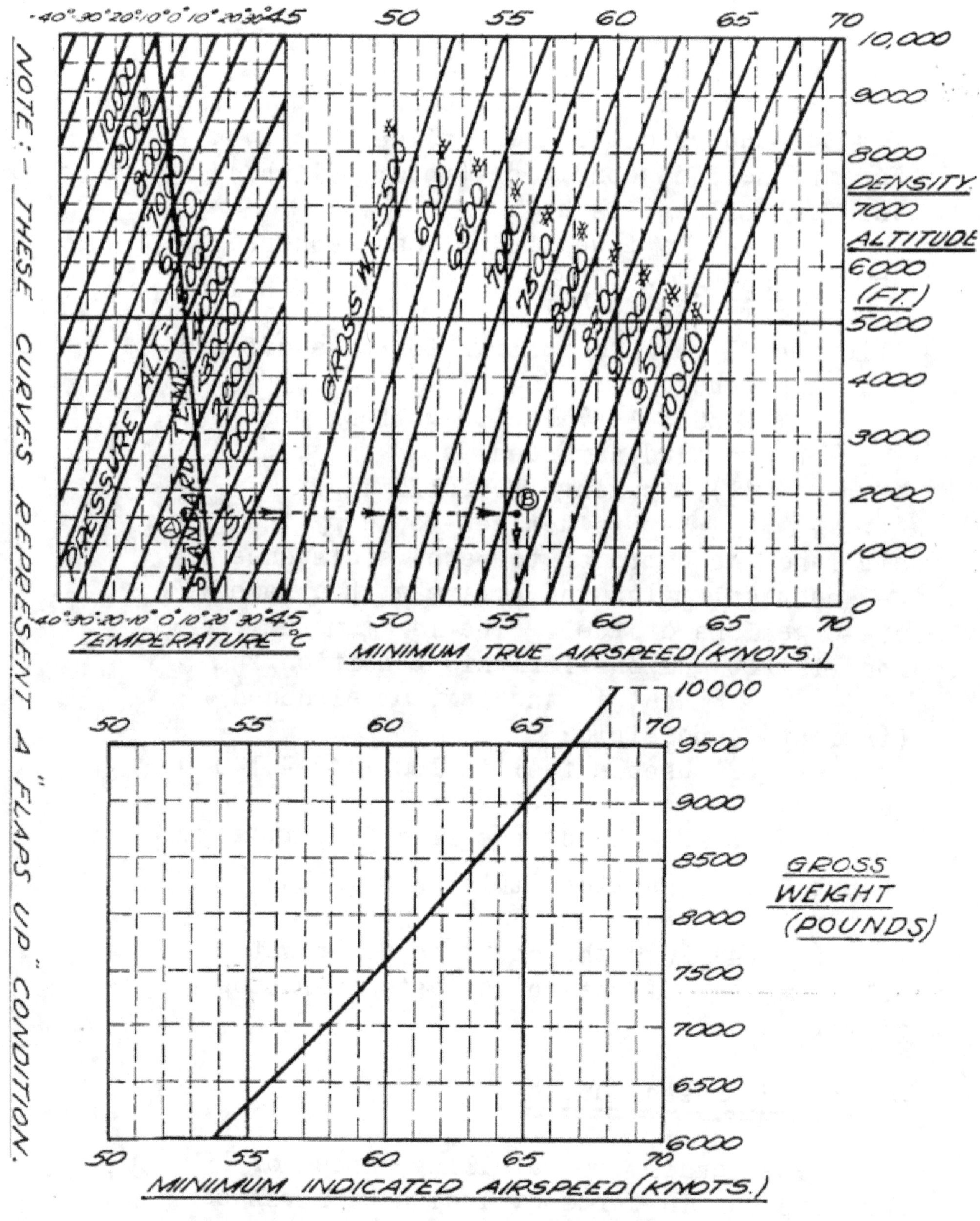

MINIMUM TRUE AIRSPEED WITHOUT POWER IS GIVEN FOR VARIOUS WEIGHTS, ALTITUDES, & TEMPERATURES. MINIMUM INDICATED AIRSPEED WITHOUT POWER IS GIVEN FOR VARIOUS WEIGHTS & IS INDEPENDENT OF ALTITUDE & TEMPERATURE.

(Airspeed Correction Chart)

When considering stalling speed in terms of
true airspeed, altitude and temperature must
be considered as stalling speed, with a given
load, increases with altitude and temperature. Chart "A" gives the true stalling airspeed for gross weights of 5500# to 10000#
corrected for temperature and altitude. An
example for the use of chart "A" follows:

2. Illustrating Use of Chart "A"

    a. Assuming the following instrument
readings:
Atmospheric temperature .... 5°C.
Altimeter .... 2100'
Gross weight .... 8250#
it is desired to know the Minimum True Stalling Airspeed.
    b. Refer to chart "A", page 93 and pro-
ceed as follows:
    (1) Enter the chart on the tempera-
ture scale in the lower left of the chart at
a point corresponding to 5°C.
    (2) Move vertically upward to a point
equal to 2100' on the sloping "pressure altitude" lines (point "A").
    (3) Go horizontally to a point cor-
responding to 8250# gross weight (point "B").
    (4) Drop down vertically and read
the true (stalling) airspeed, 55.5 knots.

F. Airspeed Correction Chart

1. The Airspeed Correction Chart provides
a means of calculating the True Airspeed,
taking into consideration the airspeed indicator reading, the altitude at which the airplane is flying and the atmospheric temperature. The curves are laid out to correct for

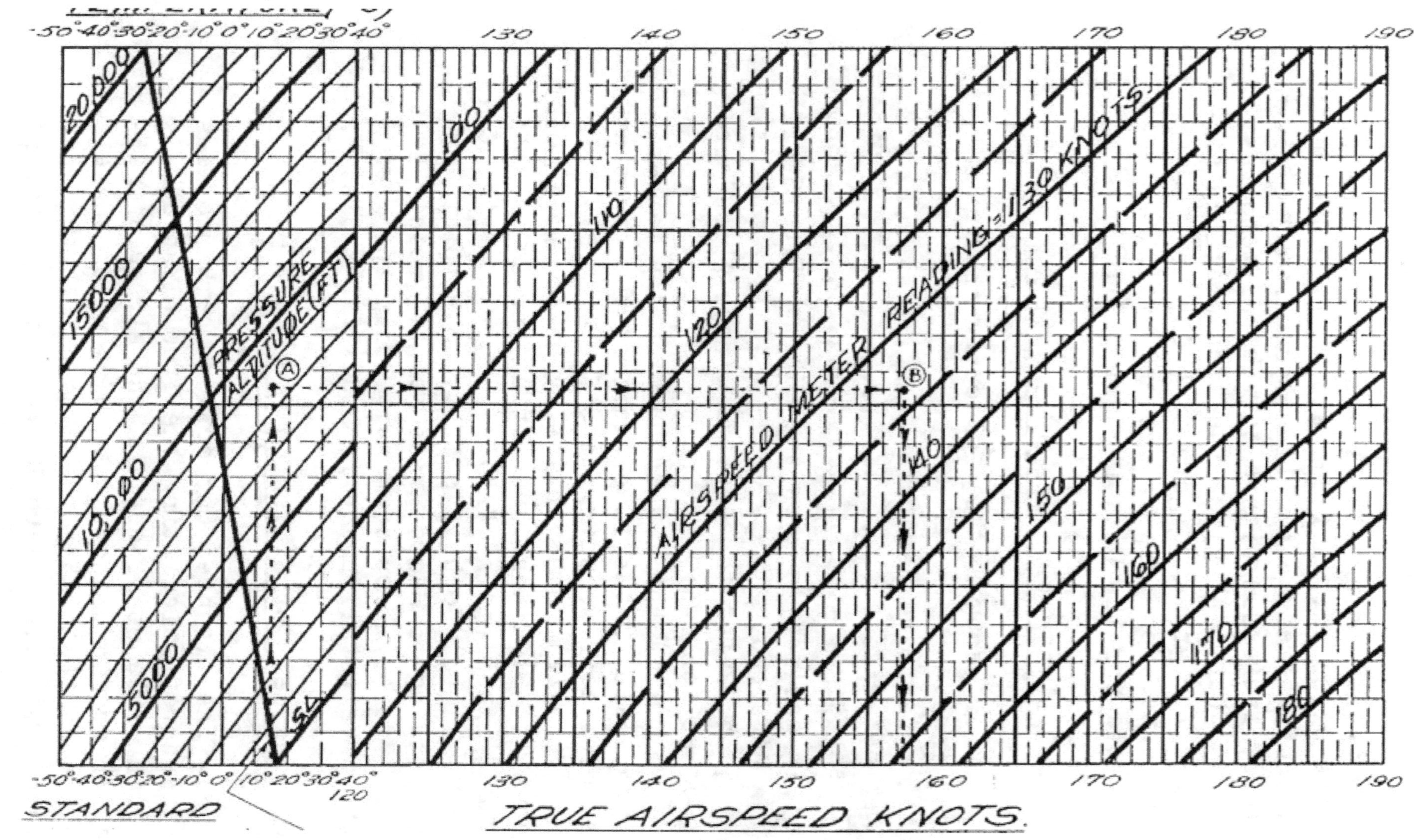
TEMPERATURE (°C)
-50° 40° 30° 20° 10° 0° 10° 20° 30° 40°
PRESSURE ALTITUDE (FT)
AIRSPEED METER READING = 130 KNOTS
20000
15000
10000
5000
SL
100
110
120
130
140
150
160
170
180
190
STANDARD
TRUE AIRSPEED KNOTS.

(Speed-Attitude Curves)

instrument error.

2. Example Illustrating Use of Chart

    a. Assuming that the following values are taken from the instruments on the airplane:

Airspeed indicator .... 134 knots
Altimeter .... 8500'
Strut temperature indicator .... 15°C.

it is desired to find the True Airspeed.

    b. Refer to Airspeed Correction Chart and proceed as follows:

    (1) Locate 15°C. on the temperature scale in the lower left hand corner of the chart.

    (2) Go vertically to a point corresponding to the indicated altitude reading of 8500' (Point A).

    (3) Continue to the right in a horizontal direction to a point corresponding to the airspeed indicator reading of 134 knots (Point B).

    (4) Drop down vertically and read the desired True Airspeed on the horizontal scale, 157.3 knots.

G. Speed-Attitude Curves

1. In making up the Speed-Attitude Curves, the angle of thrust line to flight path is shown plotted against indicated airspeed (airspeed indicator reading) for a flaps up (solid lines) and a flaps down (dotted lines) condition and for various gross weights. Indicated velocity is used because it allows for simplicity. If true airspeed were used corrections for altitude

and temperature would be required.

2. When the true airspeed is known and it is desired to know the attitude, first convert the true airspeed to indicated by using the Airspeed Correction Chart, page 95.

3. In using the curves, first select the one approximating the gross weight of the airplane as loaded. Then locate a point on that curve corresponding to the indicated airspeed. Projecting this point to the scale on the left will determine the attitude of the airplane under the given conditions.

FIGURE 4: Assistant Pilot / Bombardier's Cockpit

FIGURE 2: Bombardier's View of Pilot Cockpit

FIGURE 3: Bombardier's Position Showing Bomb Bay Doors

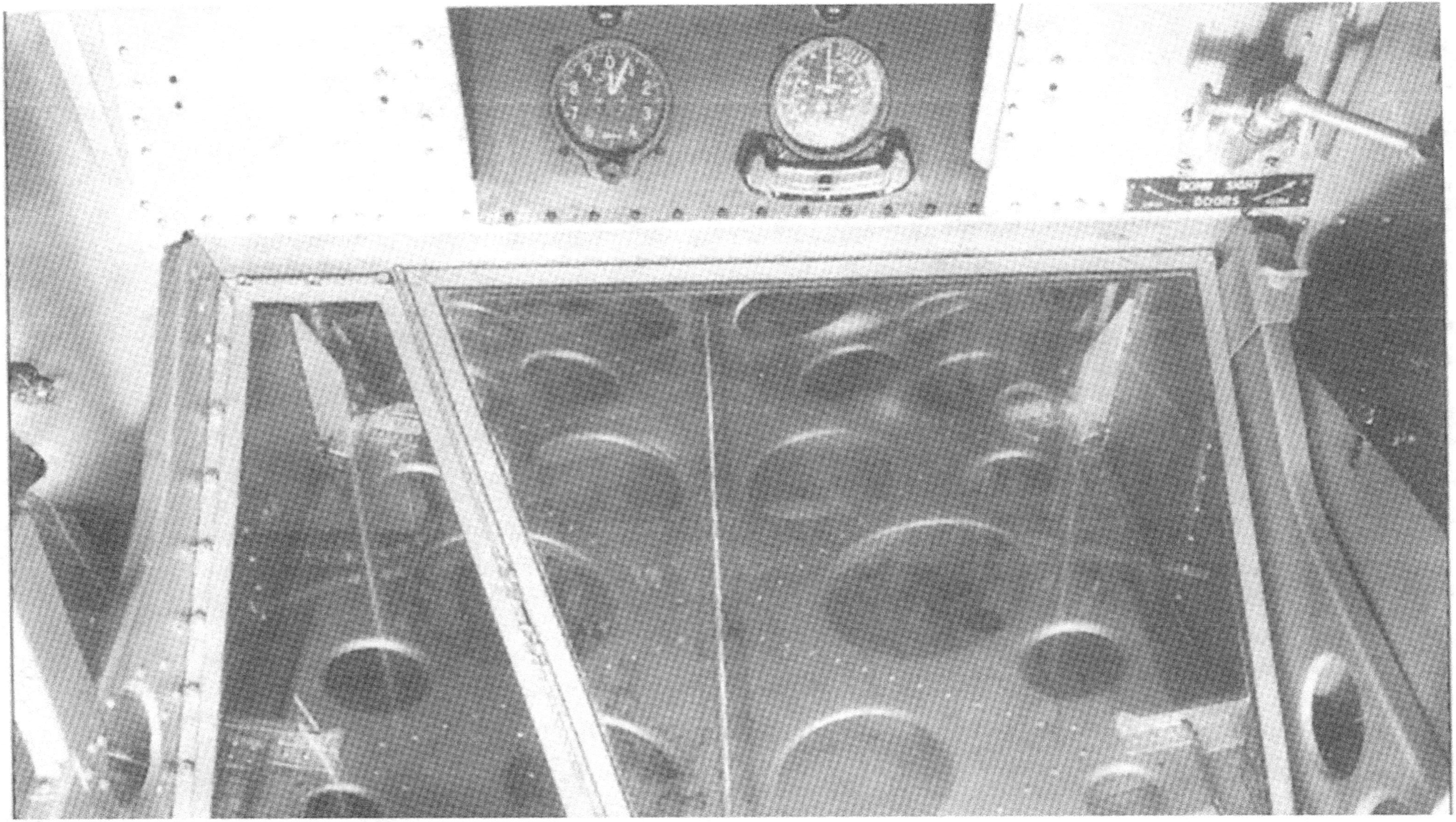

FIGURE 4: Bomb Release Handles

FIGURE 5: Assistant Pilot / Bombardier's Seat

CONFIDENTIAL FIGURE 6: Pilot's Cockpit Showing Gunsight And Torpedo Director

 FIGURE 7: Assistant Pilot Seat Showing Bombardier's Position

FIGURE 8: Radioman-Gunner's Position

FIGURE 9: Bomb Bay Doors And Bombardier's Position From Below

FIGURE 10: Bomb Bay Doors And Norden Bombsight From Interior

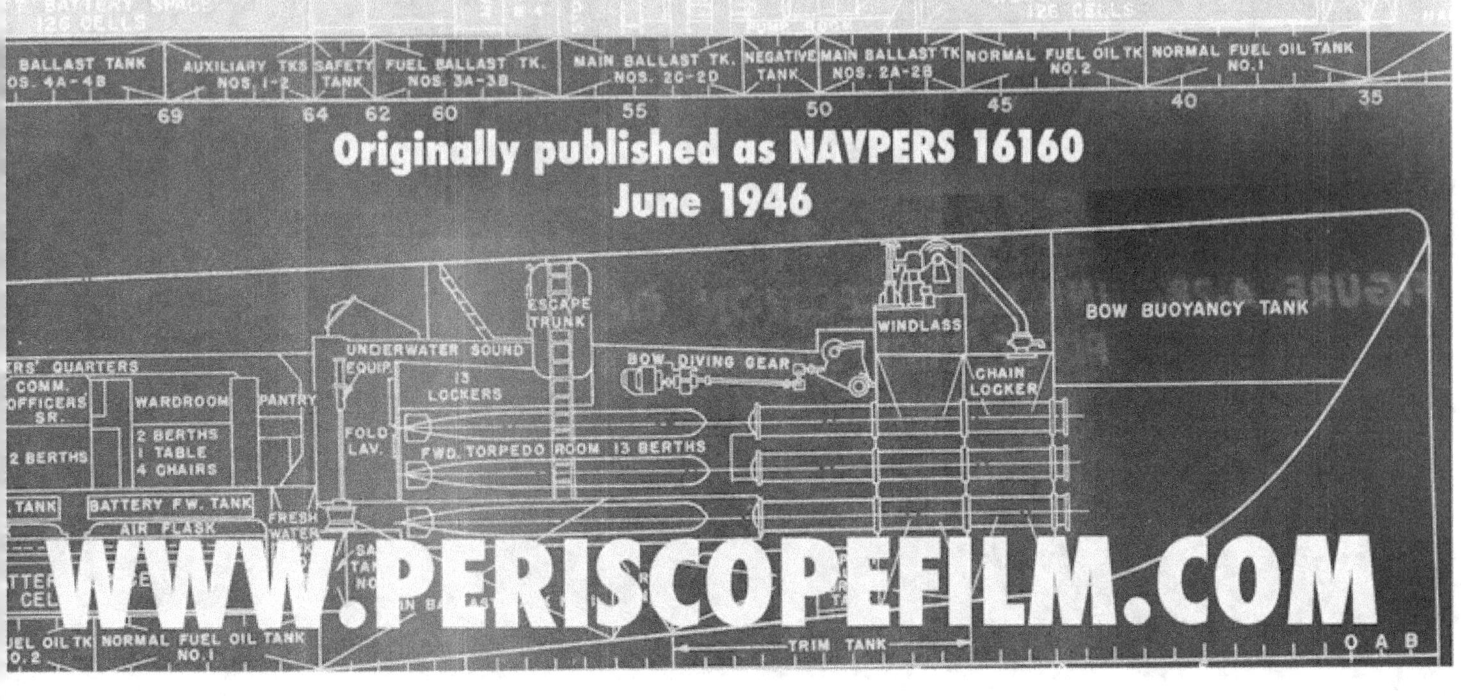

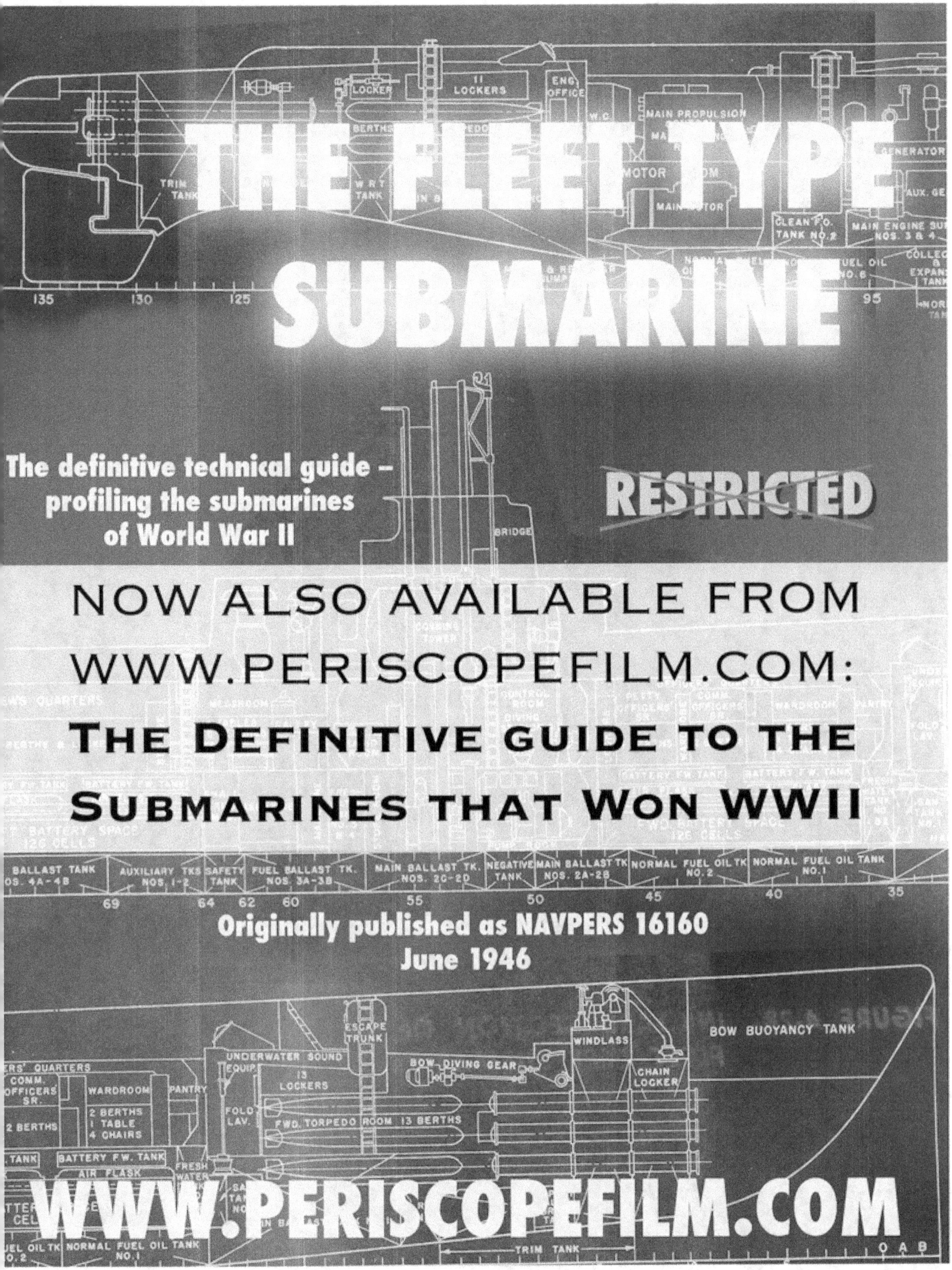

THE FLEET TYPE SUBMARINE

The definitive technical guide – profiling the submarines of World War II

RESTRICTED

NOW ALSO AVAILABLE FROM WWW.PERISCOPEFILM.COM:

THE DEFINITIVE GUIDE TO THE SUBMARINES THAT WON WWII

Originally published as NAVPERS 16160
June 1946

WWW.PERISCOPEFILM.COM

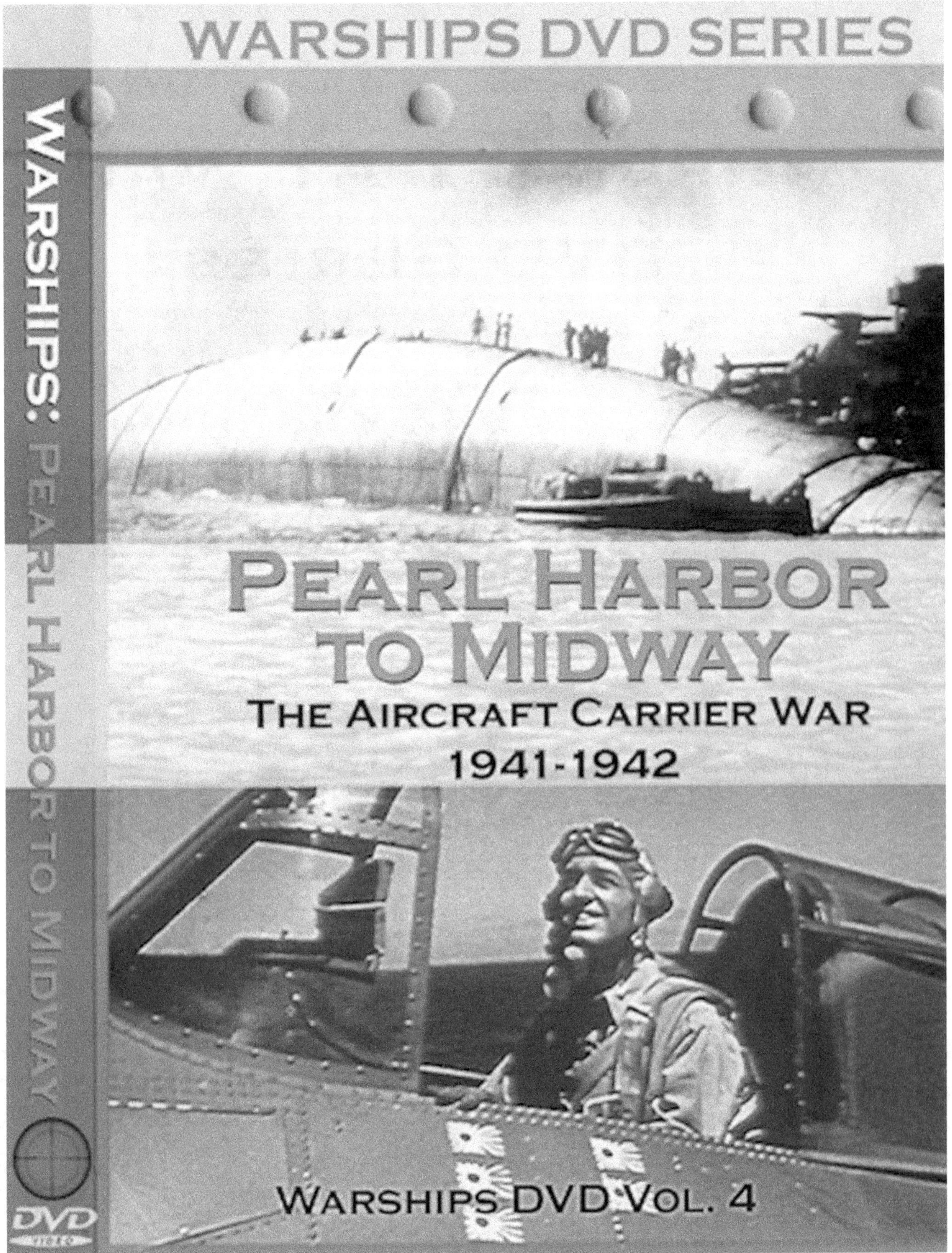

NOW AVAILABLE!

AIRCRAFT AT WAR
DVD SERIES

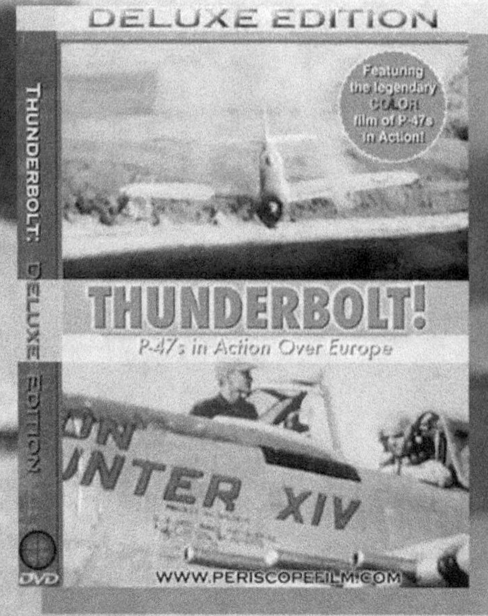

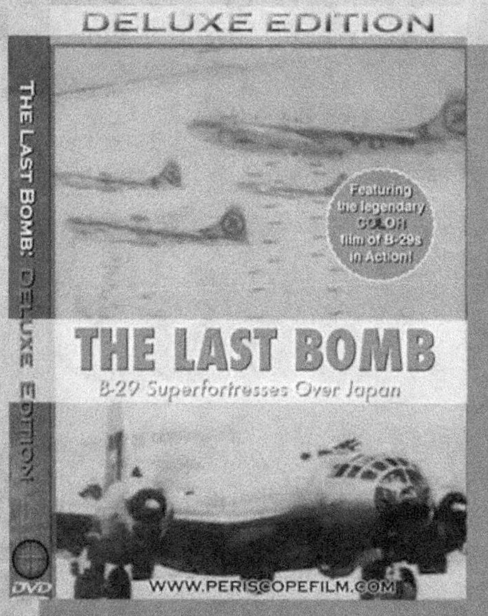

NOW AVAILABLE!

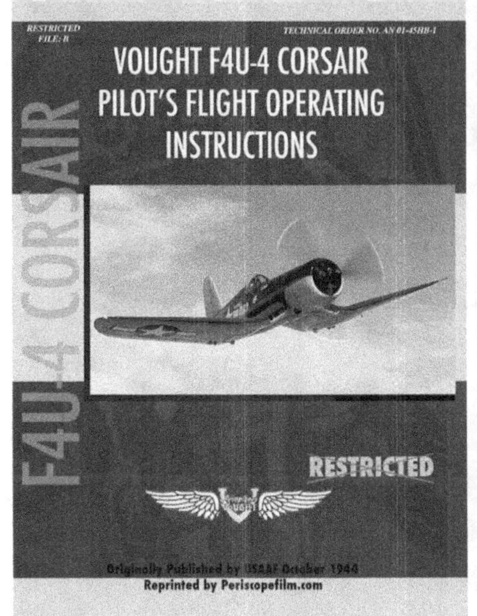

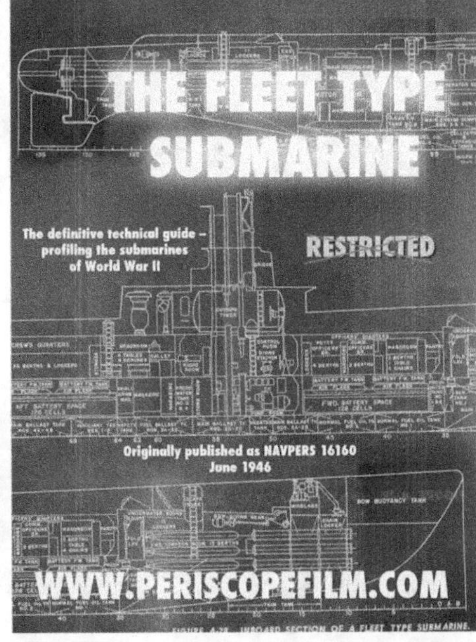

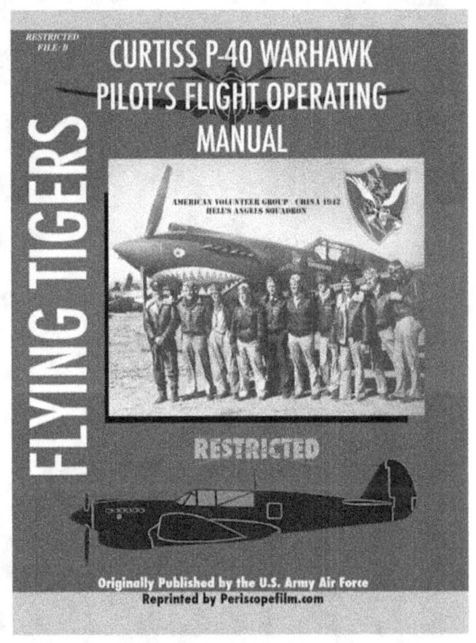

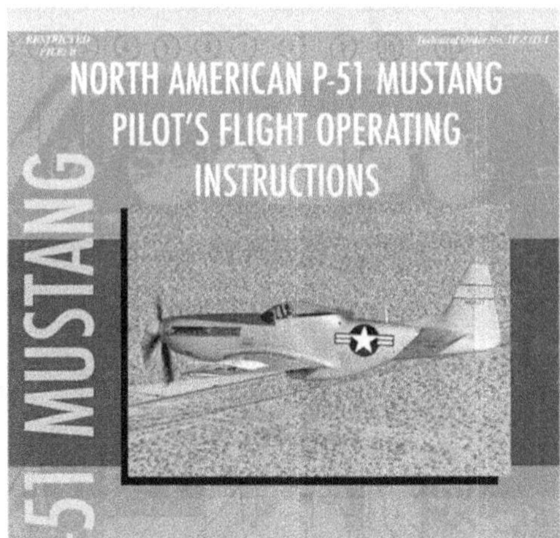

ALSO NOW AVAILABLE
FROM PERISCOPEFILM.COM